Praise for *Dark Days, Bright Nights*

"Matthew O'Brien's *Beneath the Neon* introduced the country—and so many media outlets—to the tunnels beneath Vegas and the people who lived there. How easy it would have been to play the voyeur, to just walk away. But O'Brien does what is needed. *Dark Days, Bright Nights* is an important book because it refuses to let us look away. It allows us to sit down at the metaphorical table and listen. This is the story of lives gone wrong, of people who have fallen, who are flawed and trying. They are touching and human and alive on the page. This is the story of the other side of Vegas; it is the story of what happened to America. The question for each of us: Will we play the voyeur or sit at the table?"

Charles Bock, *New York Times* **bestselling author**
of *Beautiful Children* and *Alice & Oliver*

"A profound, moving, and inspiring book about the world beneath Las Vegas and how human beings can survive and overcome the toughest challenges in life. Everyone should read this wonderful work!"

Johann Hari, author of *Chasing the Scream:*
The First and Last Days of the War on Drugs

"With the heart of an artist and the ear of a journalist, Matthew O'Brien first shined a light on the homeless people who exist in the storm tunnels of Las Vegas. In *Dark Days, Bright Nights*, O'Brien brings their heart-wrenching stories to the surface and offers us an unforgettable portrait of a slice of humanity most would never encounter."

John L. Smith, author of *The Westside Slugger:*
Joe Neal's Lifelong Fight for Social Justice

"*Dark Days, Bright Nights* is not summer reading: It's all-seasons reading, and a reader may well pull it off the shelf and read it more than once. Using the unfiltered words of the homeless in Las Vegas, Matt O'Brien has compacted, in some 240 pages, volumes of truth, the kind that sociologists can't possibly reveal in studies and statistics. Matt's interviewees are not cold statistics; they are warm humans with tales of embarrassment over failure and of pride over success. I will never look at a homeless person again and see someone with a sign pandering for money. Instead, I will see a caring heart trapped inside a human whose troubled life has been a struggle against the forces of the world and against him or herself, addiction being the greatest of those."

H. Lee Barnes, award-winning author of ten books, most recently *Life Is a Country Western Song*

"In *Dark Days, Bright Nights,* O'Brien interviews thirty-six similarly cast-off homeless, editing their stories into deftly plotted narratives of lost souls driven underground by misfortune, addiction, and abuse. Some make it out, their revelatory struggles testaments to courage, hope, and redemption. For those still there, O'Brien offers a call to action. Buying this book is a start—every copy contributes to the Shine a Light project that rescues people from this social and economic neglect that echoes so darkly beneath our American prosperity."

Douglas Unger, author of *Voices from Silence* and *Leaving the Land*

"Matthew O'Brien has expertly pieced together a compelling narrative that tells the tale of human life in the storm tunnels beneath the glitter of Las Vegas. From the dwellers' early lives to adulthood, from why they went underground to how they survived or didn't, these stories of celebration will tug at your heartstrings."

Cathy Scott, journalist and author of *The Crime Book* and *The Killing of Tupac Shakur*

DARK DAYS, BRIGHT NIGHTS

DARK DAYS, BRIGHT NIGHTS

Surviving the Las Vegas Storm Drains

Matthew O'Brien

CENTRAL RECOVERY PRESS

LAS VEGAS

Central Recovery Press (CRP) is committed to publishing exceptional materials addressing addiction treatment, recovery, and behavioral healthcare topics.

For more information, visit www.centralrecoverypress.com.

Publisher: Central Recovery Press
             3321 N. Buffalo Drive
             Las Vegas, NV 89129

Library of Congress Cataloging-in-Publication Data

Names: O'Brien, Matt (Matthew), author.
Title: Dark days, bright nights : surviving the Las Vegas storm drains /
    Matthew O'Brien.
Description: Las Vegas : Central Recovery Press, 2020.
Identifiers: LCCN 2020024686 (print) | LCCN 2020024687 (ebook)
    | ISBN 9781949481426 (paperback) | ISBN 9781949481433 (ebook)
Subjects: LCSH: Homelessness--Nevada--Las Vegas. | Underground homeless
    persons--Nevada--Las Vegas.
Classification: LCC HV4506.L37 O37 2020 (print) | LCC HV4506.L37 (ebook)
    | DDC 305.569209793135--dc23
LC record available at https://lccn.loc.gov/2020024686
LC ebook record available at https://lccn.loc.gov/2020024687

Photos by Steve Fanell. Photo of Matthew O'Brien courtesy of Gilberto Campos.

Portions of the epilogue were originally published in May 2017 on dtlv.com.

Portions of Jazz's interview originally aired in August 2016 on Nevada Public Radio's *State of Nevada*.

Every attempt has been made to contact copyright holders. If copyright holders have not been properly acknowledged, please contact us. Central Recovery Press will be happy to rectify the omission in future printings of this book.

Cover by The Book Designers and interior design and layout by Sara Streifel.

To Sharon
and all of the others
who didn't make it out.

TABLE OF CONTENTS

INTRODUCTION

Seventeen years later, I still recall the scene. I was sitting at my bulky wooden desk in the office of *Las Vegas CityLife*, a now defunct alt-weekly newspaper. It was late afternoon. Thumbing through the *Las Vegas Review-Journal* in the natural light afforded by a floor-to-ceiling window, I stopped at a story about Timmy "T.J." Weber, an accused rapist and double-murderer who had been captured after three weeks on the run. The final paragraph of the story, which explained that he had used the underground flood channels to evade the police, captured my imagination.

I laid the paper on the desk and wondered what Weber experienced in the tunnels. What he saw, heard, smelled. Did clues pertaining to his crime remain? Could he hear the police dogs howling overhead?

I also wondered what lurked beneath Las Vegas. What secrets did the storm drains keep? What discoveries waited in the dark?

As the managing editor, I wasn't the person to answer those questions; I was shackled to my desk. Only the most daring and desperate mercenary would accept the assignment I had in mind, so I picked up the phone and pitched the idea of exploring the drains to *CityLife* contributor Josh Ellis, who'd displayed brass balls in his weekly column and a flair for first-person narratives in his features. To my moderate surprise he said, "Sure. Why not?"

A few weeks after he accepted the assignment, I called Josh to see how it was going. He explained how, armed with an eighteen-inch knife and accompanied by a photographer friend, he'd explored a drain that began downtown and ended at the Las Vegas Wash more than three miles away. They didn't encounter anyone, but they did see clothing and sleeping bags hanging in the manhole shafts—storage spaces, they assumed, for homeless people living aboveground near the manholes.

I asked Josh if he'd explored other drains. He hadn't, but hoped to over the weekend. "I may need a lift," he added. I agreed to pick him up that Saturday morning, stipulating that I'd serve as chauffeur, but I had no intention of entering the drains.

However, curious about what lurked beyond the shade line and not wanting to be labeled a cowardly editor, I ended up following him into a pipe in the southeast valley and two drains in the southwest. Over the next few months we explored three more drains. The "research" resulted in a co-written series that was published in *CityLife* in the summer of 2002. It was well-received locally and nationally and went viral before that term entered the lexicon. *CityLife* nominated it for the Pulitzer Prize in feature writing.

If that had marked the end of my storm-drain saga, I would've been satisfied. But it was only the beginning.

Josh and I considered turning the stories into a book, but he was moving to San Francisco, we had different visions for its style and scope, and, having heard of married couples who got divorced while working on book projects together, we figured we'd kill each other before completing the manuscript. He passed the project off to me with the understanding that if I got a book deal, I'd cut him in on the advance. Vegas-based Huntington Press commissioned the project and I gave Josh his share, and, in the summer of 2004, I took a sabbatical from *CityLife* and explored the storm-drain system on my own. These solo descents provided the foundation for *Beneath the Neon: Life and Death in the Tunnels of Las Vegas*, which was published in 2007.

One reason I wrote *Beneath the Neon* was to call attention to the fact that people live in the drains. My greatest hope was that a government agency or nonprofit would help them. My worst fear was that the cops would sweep them out. Neither was realized, so in the spring of 2009 I contacted HELP of Southern Nevada, a charity that serves the poor and homeless. "I know the drains and the people in them," I explained in an email to HELP's management. "You have the resources and know-how. Perhaps we can work together?" A few weeks later I began escorting HELP's social workers into the underworld, and Shine a Light—a community project that provides housing, counseling, and other services to those in the drains—was born.

Part of Shine a Light's mission is to raise awareness of the people in the drains and advocate on their behalf. One way I've done this is through the media (while, of course, promoting my book). When *Beneath the Neon* was released, I reached out to media outlets and received a generous amount of coverage, but within weeks I no longer needed to contact them; they were contacting me. This was, in part, due to the recession. The economy tanked and Vegas became the poster child of the boom and bust. Media from around the world (the ones who still had a job) fixated on "Sin City," and, during their research, the tunnels would inevitably come up and they'd request a tour. If they were serious journalists (i.e., not tabloid hacks) and willing to make a donation to Shine a Light or buy supplies for the people we interviewed, I'd agree to play Virgil to their Dante and guide them through this inferno. These stipulations scared off some journalists, but most moved forward. *Nightline*, *Dr. Phil*, the *New York Times*, CNN, the BBC, *Al Jazeera*, *Le Monde*, and *Der Spiegel*—they and many more descended with me into the tunnels (though, citing ethics, not all donated to the cause).

I visited the tunnels on behalf of Shine a Light and/or the media at least once every two weeks, and I performed duties related to the community project—communicating with social workers, picking up donations, fielding media requests—on a daily basis. This continued until July 2017, when I moved to El Salvador to teach. However, before leaving Las Vegas, I made sure to do two things: find a way to keep Shine a Light alive and interview people who made it out of the drains.

With support from Shine a Light, HELP of Southern Nevada, U.S. VETS, and others, several people found their way out of the storm drains and were reintegrating into society. I knew many of them; some I considered friends. Over coffee, on the phone, or through Facebook, I gathered snippets of their stories about childhood, homelessness, discovering the drains, getting out and getting clean, and lessons learned, and I was struck by how compelling and inspiring the stories were and how skilled they were at telling them. I wanted to share what I'd heard. I felt obligated to. *Beneath the Neon* showed the dark side of homelessness in Las Vegas, people at their lowest, literally and figuratively. It only seemed fair to tell the other side of the story—the happy ending I could never have envisioned when Josh and I first stumbled into the drains.

My goal wasn't to talk to everyone who made it out. I wanted diversity in age, ethnicity, gender, sexual orientation, drug of choice, and length of time in the drains. When I'd done all that I could to reach that goal, I'd interviewed thirty-six people. The conversations took place between January 2017 and April 2019. I asked each person the same questions in the same order: "What's your earliest memory? What was your childhood like? Where'd you go to high school and what kind of student were you? What'd you do after high school?" When I finished an interview, which usually took one to two hours, I'd transcribe it, then schedule the next one.

Shortly into the interview process, I realized I had a lot of interesting content, but I wasn't sure how to structure it. I considered monologues, but more than thirty of them? That would be overkill. So which ten to fifteen people would I focus on? There were so many worthy subjects and powerful stories.

Looking for guidance, I emailed a handful of writer friends, explaining the project and its structural possibilities. My former *CityLife* collaborator, Josh Ellis, thought a collage of oral accounts might work well, and he loaned me his copy of *Please Kill Me: The Uncensored Oral History of Punk* to serve as a model. My book began to take shape. I turned the questions I'd asked the subjects into chapter headings, included the most memorable responses in each chapter, and edited and arranged the stories to give them a narrative flow. *Dark Days, Bright Nights: Surviving the Las Vegas Storm Drains* is the result.

My role with Shine a Light is a middleman of sorts between the people in the drains and those who want to help them. That, essentially, is the role I play in this book. These survivors shared their stories with me and I'm passing them on to you. The book, however, does not venture to tell thirty-six individual narratives, but one overarching tale—a tapestry of homelessness in America and life in and out of the tunnels of Las Vegas. I also hope it busts some myths about homelessness and provides a unique perspective on the city. And 25 percent of the book's proceeds will benefit Shine a Light, which was folded into the Las Vegas Freedom House Sober Living center when I moved to Central America.

What if I had not read the *Review-Journal* on that fateful day in 2002? What if I didn't finish reading the story about Timmy "T.J." Weber being captured? Or the reporter had not included the paragraph about Weber's underground escape? I wonder what path my career would've taken and what my life would look like now. The storm drains have become a part of who I am, and the former residents have proven to be the most honest and loyal people I've met in Las Vegas, which is more of a compliment to them than a slight to the city. I don't, however, presume to speak for them. As this book attests, they do that quite well themselves.

Matthew O'Brien
April 2019

DISCOVERING THE DRAINS PART I

To understand the landscape of the Las Vegas Valley, as I explained in my book *Beneath the Neon*, simply look at the palm of your hand. The mounds on the perimeter of the palm are the mountain ranges surrounding the valley. The concave interior is the basin floor. The lines are flood channels, the more prominent ones primary washes that widen and deepen over time.

Like a palm, the valley is enclosed except for a shallow groove in a bottom corner. The Las Vegas Wash, which marks the basin's lowest elevation, drains through this groove into Lake Mead.

Located in the heart of the Mojave—the driest desert in North America—Las Vegas is lethally hot and arid. Its average high temperature in June, July, and August is 102 degrees Fahrenheit. The average yearly rainfall is only four inches, most of which falls during the so-called monsoon season, when Vegas is susceptible to flash floods. The asphalt, concrete, and hardpan desert soil absorb little water. The slopes of the basin carry it onto streets and into natural flood channels, toward the Las Vegas Wash, at speeds exceeding twenty-five miles per hour.

In 1985, after a series of floods crippled Las Vegas, the state legislature created the Clark County Regional Flood Control District. The goal was to reduce flooding by building a network of channels. It was Southern Nevada's first coordinated attempt to control flooding, which had only been done piecemeal by various entities, including Clark County, Las Vegas, and North Las Vegas.

Along with the Las Vegas Valley, which grew from a population of 750,000 in 1990 to more than two million people, the flood system is constantly expanding. The intricate web spans from mountain range to mountain range, like the lines on a palm, and currently consists of eighty detention basins and 600 miles of channel, roughly half of which are underground.

Despite these figures—and the crucial role the drains play in the city's functionality—the flood channels are not a prominent feature of Vegas's landscape or lore. They lie low, in off-the-beaten-path places, blocked off by walls and chainlink fences or camouflaged by the beige desert floor.

Which begs the question, "How did you discover the storm drains?"

Szmauz, 24, a rock musician from the mountains of New Hampshire, had a violent and unforgettable introduction to the drains: I was giving this other homeless guy hot dogs I'd found in a dumpster near Tropicana and McLeod, and out of the corner of my eye I see this big guy come over and he decks me. The hot dogs go flying. I was stunned. It took me a second to realize I just got hit in the face.

He starts wailing on me and I fight back. I'm not a small guy, so he took off.

I had this meat cleaver on me and I'm chasing him down the street with it. The drug dealers that lived in the shitty apartments nearby knew me. I was a loyal customer of theirs. They were like, "Dude, what's up?"

I said, "Get that guy!"

We're all chasing him and he dipped through a hole in a fence and went down into a wash and into a tunnel. We all stopped. We're like, We're not going in there!

And that's how I discovered the tunnels.

Barry, 48, a sex offender from Howell, Michigan, came to Las Vegas after an eighteen-year incarceration: In prison I'd seen that show *Modern Marvels* on the History Channel and they talked about the flood channels, so when I got to Vegas I just walked around town looking for 'em. Down past the "Welcome" sign I found one and figured I'd check it out.

It was dark, scary. I was wondering who I'd meet. Any decent people or just rats, spiders, and trash. I had a flashlight on me. I always carry one.

That's when I ran into Kregg. He'd lived down there a while and they called him "The Mayor." He had a wall of plastic up and I knocked on it and talked to him for a couple minutes. Told him my name, where I was from, what I was in prison for, and his response was, "There's room farther down to make a camp, but don't tell no one what you were in prison for."

Manny, 47, a member of the Tlingit Indian Tribe in Alaska, lived in the tunnels for ten years: I knew about the ones by the Rio. Me and a girlfriend had stayed in them when we were young. I didn't mind it because I was with her and we had one foot in and one out. We were just kids having fun.

But in 2001 I got into a fight. This dude was looking at me and I was looking at him, then he started talking shit. I was a young man and he was an older guy, and I beat him down. I thought that was it. I went to get a drink in Mermaids casino and I come out, and I feel someone crack me from the side with a beer bottle.

I stumbled down to Bonneville Avenue. My tank top was soaked with blood. That's as far as I got before I passed out.

When I woke up in the hospital the doctor said, "There's a chance you're going to lose sight in that eye."

"What are the chances?"

"Ninety-nine percent."

I ended up getting several stitches and I lost sight in my left eye.

When I was released I went to a buddy's house, but I didn't want to be a burden and I didn't feel like hustling wearing an eye patch. That's when I went back into the drains.

Ricky Lee, 53, lived in the tunnels off and on from 1995 to 2016, and is part ruffian, part poet: I was living in an abandoned hotel, but I was working. I was handing out smut on the Strip. The hotel owner would come by every once in a while and kick me out. I told him, "I got a job. How 'bout I pay you for the room?"

He said that'd be fine, so I gave him eighty dollars a week.

I saw the tunnels being built not far from the hotel, and I had always admired the TV show *Beauty and the Beast*. That guy Vincent lived in tunnels and I wanted to do that too.

Half Pint, 58, from western Nebraska, got her street name because of her diminutive stature: My first night on the streets I slept behind a dumpster at 7-Eleven, then I walked and ended up at Desert Breeze Park. I was so fucked up on pills. I woke up at the park tied to a bench, half naked. I had no idea what happened.

I kept walking and somebody told me I could go down into this culvert, an open flood plain by the Orleans casino. There were three big tunnels and I went in the middle one and was immediately met by all sorts of spiders and weird smells. It was really dark and my eyes had to adjust. I passed out.

When I woke there were other people there. "Hey, you all right? What are you doing here?"

One of the guys said, "You can't stay here and puke all over our stuff. Get outta here!"

I started crying and he had a moment of sympathy. He said, "You don't look like you belong here."

"I don't." I gave him a sob story and he offered me a crack pipe.

RICKY LEE

Tex, 46, is a funny, friendly Army vet who described his twelve years in the drains with a thick Southern drawl: When you're in Vegas and homeless, the best thing for you is not to be seen. Vegas doesn't like homeless people and the police harass you, so I found me a tunnel and made it my home. There's a homeless person on just about every corner and one of 'em showed me the spot.

SHAGGY

Shaggy, 29, was a heroin addict in the tunnels from 2011 to 2014. His mom, One Shoe Sue, also lived in the drains: I was going back and forth by bus between Summerlin and Henderson. It'd take about three hours. I'd panhandle and make 100 bucks, and I kept my backpack and sleeping bag on me and I'd crash wherever I landed.

Eventually a few guys from the tunnels saw me panhandling near Eastern Avenue and the 215. They actually challenged me. They tried to get me to move from my spot. They said my time was up, but I wouldn't leave.

Later that day they sought me out and said, "Hey, man. You got heart. You should come down with us where you're safe and out of the way."

Stephen, 62, was born and raised in Las Vegas. A longtime waiter and maître d', he found himself living under Paradise Road near the Hard Rock Hotel: I just woke up one day and was living, or I should say dying, in the tunnels under Paradise.

EARLIEST MEMORY

On any given night in the United States, 568,000 people find themselves without a fixed, adequate residence, according to the Department of Housing and Urban Development's 2019 annual report on homelessness. Of those individuals, 30 percent are in families with children, 7 percent are veterans, and 6 percent are under the age of twenty-five. People of color are overrepresented on the street compared to their numbers in the general population. Native Americans, who make up 1 percent of the population, are 3 percent of the homeless; Hispanics, 18 percent of the population, are 22 percent of the homeless; and African-Americans, 13 percent of the population, are 40 percent of the homeless.

Despite these sad and sobering statistics, and the high visibility of the homeless in most major U.S. cities, the issue goes largely ignored. What little media attention it garners often lacks depth. Reporters, most of whom have no personal experience with homelessness, tend to tell the story from the perspective of politicians, social-service organizations, and individual activists. If they do interview a homeless person, their questions, at best, focus on the immediate past, the present, and the near future: "How did you become homeless? How do you survive on the streets? What would it take to get you housed?" Precious little coverage—mine included—delves deep into the person's backstory to find clues to help solve the mystery that is homelessness.

"What's your earliest memory? Describe your childhood and high school years. What did you do after high school?" These prompts inform the chapters "Earliest Memory," "Childhood," and "Adulthood." I wondered if there were commonalities in how the interviewees were raised and educated. Was their homelessness foreshadowed? Are there root causes of the issue? In short, I was curious if anything in their background might help explain how they ended up in the storm drains of Las Vegas.

Cyndi, 50, lived in the drains for three years with her husband Rick. An alcoholic and a meth addict, she lost custody of her five children and traces a lot of her problems to a tragic early memory: When I was two, my baby brother fell off the bunk bed and snapped his neck and died. That haunted me for a long time because I was supposed to be watching him. I considered myself a murderer from that age on. My father committed suicide on my brother's birthday the next year, so I felt like I had killed two people by the time I was three years old.

Four Finger Mike, 61, who lost part of four fingers in a middle school shop-class accident, recalled one of America's darkest days: My mom took us out of school when John F. Kennedy got assassinated. Mom and Dad had taken me and my sister to the old Las Vegas convention center to watch Kennedy speak just two months before that. My mom taught at J.D. Smith middle school and I was across the street at C.P. Squires elementary with my sister, and when he got killed they closed the schools and my mom came and got us. We went home and watched the news on a black-and-white TV. Walter Cronkite.

Ande, 59, who has a doctorate in organizational behavior and human factors, lived in the drains for seven years, the last while battling breast cancer. Her earliest memory is also related to JFK's assassination: They were doing the twenty-one-gun salute—boom! boom! boom!—and I was glued to the TV. My mother said, "Wouldn't it be funny if a duck fell from the sky?" I turned around and she was standing there with her apron on. I remember thinking, I can't believe she just said that! She had to break the seriousness of the situation, and it was the funniest thing I'd ever heard.

Becky, 33, lived in the tunnels for two years with her boyfriend Zero. She grew up in Southern California: I guess because I had seen my mom snorting meth, I found some drywall on the carpet and chopped it up on the mirror and made little lines. That was my pretend play. Meth was always in the house—my mom was an addict and the guy who raised me sold dope—and it just carried over to me.

Phil, 47, a former crack addict, lived in the drains for nine years: An adoption agency. I think I was four or five. I remember sitting in an indoor sandbox, waiting.

Easy E, 47, lived in the drains for nine years, like his good friend Phil. He shared a memory that foreshadowed his struggles with meth and alcohol: I was five years old and my new parents had an adoption party for me. It was in Hurleyville, New York, in the middle of August, and it was about ninety degrees and 100 percent humidity. I was wearing blue Mickey Mouse sunglasses. I remember there was a bottle of beer, Genesee Cream Ale, and I watched the sweat run down the side of it and I was thirsty, so I drank some. There was three or four people around, including my new father, and everybody started laughing, so I finished it. When nobody was looking I found another and drank it too.

My mom and dad found me several hours later in the sandbox, covered in puke and surrounded by beer bottles. I had laid the bottles on their side to try to hide them. I honestly believe my addiction started then, because I even tried to hide the liquor.

Merch, 59, got his street name by stealing merchandise, which he often bartered for drugs. He lived in the drains for ten years, despite an idyllic upbringing in Dayton, Ohio: My father belonged to a Masonic temple. They marched in parades across the country and I was the mascot. I wore a fez with puffy pants, bright colors, and a sash. I carried a sword and marched with the group. We would do different maneuvers throughout the parade. We marched in Baltimore, Philadelphia, St. Louis, a lot of cities.

Manny: A black-and-white kitten. I threw it off a two-story building to see if it could fly. It landed on its feet and was fine. I guess I was a hostile child.

Misty, 35, grew up in foster homes throughout Oregon, but occasionally lived with her alcoholic mother and her mom's assorted partners: My birth mother had gotten married to this guy Roger. He used to sit there and take flies and dip 'em in water, then pour salt on 'em and watch 'em try to fly away. There was something really wrong with that dude.

Shaggy: Waking up in the middle of the night in Arizona. I think it was Phoenix. I was in first or second grade. My mom told me to grab what I could, that we were leaving. That was a constant for me and my mom. She was a prostitute and crack addict and we moved from place to place.

Half Pint: I have a lot of memories of being rejected. My dad was a politician for twenty-five years in Nebraska and he often went on the campaign trail. Votes counted. I was the kid that went to the grandparents' or the babysitter's, that didn't usually go campaigning. I had twin brothers that were younger than me. They were the golden children.

I remember going to Lincoln for an event and driving eight hours cross-state, Mom and Dad bitching at me the whole way. "We really need you to be present at this one. Everyone needs to be there."

I was fighting with my brothers, and my dad would pull over and beat me. We finally got there and he looked at me and said, "You're ruining my life! I don't know why we even had you!"

Melinda, 44, lived in the drains for two years with her boyfriend Manny. An alcoholic, she lost custody of her five children, and was herself raised by a single mother: Waiting for my mom to come home. I'd hardly see her because she always worked. I missed her and would wait for her early in the morning. She was a cocktail waitress and worked the graveyard shift, and that'd be the only time I could see her. She was either out with a boyfriend or at work or school. Sometimes she'd go on trips and leave me for weeks at a time or drop me off at my grandma and grandpa's.

Vegas Dee, 43, lived in the tunnels for two years with her boyfriend Ned. She recalled snippets of a violent childhood: When I was a little older I started having memories of what happened to me, and they dated back to when I was two.

I had a memory that I'd suppressed. Frankfurt, Germany. I was in a crib. I can still see the house: a big velvet Jesus on the wall and the clean, wood stairs.

My parents were total opposites. My dad can be a witty, smart guy. He was in the military. My mom was very religious. She was compassionate and caring.

I remember him smacking her across the room. I also remember my dad not knowing why he did what he did to her and us. There's no way to explain it. It's just something he chose to do to me and my sister.

Ricky Lee: I remember my brother being born. I remember the TVs and radios we used to watch and listen to together. I remember those football games that would shake and the players would move across the field.

I try not to remember too much more than that because I start to get mad.

Zero, 46, lived in the tunnels for two years with his girlfriend Becky. He grew up in southern Louisiana: I have flashes of memory from before I was ten. I have a lotta shit blocked out, I guess. I remember when I was nine my mom had a birthday party for me at McDonald's. It was by my grandparents' house in Metairie, Louisiana, and we lived in Kenner, and all my friends from both places showed up. I hadn't seen my mom for two years prior to that, because she had moved to Ohio and took my sister with her.

My friend Derrick gave me a Dallas Cowboys frisbee. That's the only present I remember. There was a birthday cake. The McDonald's was nice. It was one of the first that was bigger and in a strip mall. This was the late seventies. High-class shit back then. When McDonald's had some pride.

Ned, 38, lived in the drains for two years with his girlfriend Vegas Dee: Christmas Day. My entire family at my grandmother's house in Chicago. Probably forty individuals. One of my uncles dressed as Santa and one my cousins dressed as an elf. There was a huge tree in the front room and the room was packed with gifts from the tree all the way to door, two feet deep. After dinner my uncle and cousin distributed the gifts.

The new Nintendo was out. I didn't get that, but one of my aunties gave me the original Atari, the 2600, with the wood paneling, red button, and black joystick.

My dad left when I was young, but before that we went to Toys R Us and he bought me a He-Man bike. He-Man was a big thing for me.

I remember my dad was behind me and so was my mom. They were trying to keep me steady. I started to get some balance. I was pedaling faster and faster, and they kept encouraging me, and I didn't realize they had let go because I was looking forward. When I looked back and realized no one was behind me, I crashed.

CHILDHOOD

Ande: My whole family was from Chicago. My dad dated Al Capone's little sister. Then one day he was reading a newspaper and learned about Disneyland opening, and he thought California was going to boom, specifically this city called Anaheim. He moved there and coaxed both sides of the family to join him. We lived near Knott's Berry Farm and I was born at Fullerton hospital. They brought me home on Christmas Eve.

I knew a lot of people in high school, but I was a loner. I didn't know I was gay. I had a station wagon—I was popular because of it—and was a straight-A student who didn't give a fuck. I was too advanced for high school. I didn't attend many classes. All I did was edit the yearbook.

They tried to expel me because I didn't take part in PE. I'm like, "You're outta your mind! I'm not going to wear leotards and jump over leather horses or do ballet!" I just sat on the bleachers in my school uniform and did math and pissed off everybody.

My friends and I went to see *Emmanuelle: The Joys of a Woman*, and they all turned to me and said, "You're going to be gay within a year."

I was like, "What? Is there a magic potion that makes you gay? How do you know that?"

We went on a lot of trips in my station wagon—camping, to waterfalls and rivers—and we had a blast, but they could tell I was different.

Misty: I was born drunk. My mother was shit-faced and puking when she had me. I had fetal alcohol syndrome.

She would've had eleven of us, but she had a couple miscarriages. The only sibling I knew, the one I grew up with, was my brother Cody. We're a year apart.

My mom and my stepfather John were drinking one night and arguing. I heard them and got up to see what was going on. He was coming at her with a knife, so I jumped in between them and he stabbed me in the arm. I was eight at the time. I wasn't hurt too bad, but it left a scar.

Mom and John stayed together awhile. Ups and downs and everything in between. At one point they were homeless and living in a wooded area behind the laundromat and the church. My brother and I would sneak out of our foster home and visit their camp.

I was on drugs and ended up at Rosemont girls school in Portland. That place was crazy. We started riots there. Getting carried by six big staffers into a padded cell while wearing a straitjacket. It was like a minimum-security prison, a juvie lock-up.

My brother Cody and I met our birth father once, and he was supposed to come back to see us. He kept promising to, but never did. We found out later, when we were staying with a foster family, that he died. The foster parents took us to find his gravesite somewhere in Salem. They said he either died five miles outside of Salem in a ditch by the road or behind a building in Portland when it was cold out.

He wasn't homeless. Had a wife, kids, a place to stay. I don't know the full story. We never did find his grave.

Maddie, 19, met her boyfriend Knyck in the tunnels. A former heroin addict, she was born and raised in Las Vegas, and ended up underground after running away from home: When my dad remarried I had an evil stepmom. She was abusive. She told me that my mom was a bad person and I was going to be fat and lazy like her. When I was eight she told me that she looked better in a bikini than I did. She was really fucked up and created a lot of problems for me.

My mom was a vice president for the Venetian casino in the accounting department. She's a workaholic. She'd go to work at six in the morning and wouldn't come back till four, then she'd go straight to the bar to drink and gamble.

When I was ten, I started drinking and smoking cigarettes. Around that same time I was raped by my stepmom's brother. I told my dad and he tried to talk to him, but he said we were just wrestling.

I met Olivia in middle school. She was the only other tall chick, so I was drawn to her. She was a punk-rocker. I wasn't able to dress myself before then or have friends, so I liked how she looked. She had freedom and expression and I thought, Maybe I can learn from her.

She introduced me to a lot of music: the Sex Pistols, the Misfits, Mayhem. Before that I was trying to be a wigger. We'd hang out and go to her house and drink and do pills. She thought it was cool to be punk and eat out of trashcans.

Then she met Jabber Jaw in the Henderson area, where we'd go to drink, and he showed us the tunnels.

Cyndi: After my baby brother died and my father committed suicide, I went to church and tried every religion I could find. I wanted to make sure they went to heaven. All the churches said that since my brother had not been baptized he was going to hell and since my dad committed suicide he was going too. In my young, twisted mind I thought since I killed them they'd go to heaven and I'd go to hell.

I played hooky a lot and dropped out in the ninth grade. I didn't like school because I have learning disabilities. In the seventies they didn't know how to deal with someone like me. I needed a different kind of teaching than they could provide.

Merch: Dayton, Ohio. Very uneventful and stress free. Mom and Dad didn't drink. There was never any domestic violence. They bought a house in the country in '66. Perfect childhood really.

My dad woke up one Saturday with a headache. He went into a coma the next day and three days later died. He was thirty-eight. I was twelve.

It was tough. My mom took care of me and my sister. To this day she's never been with another man.

"Your dad was the man I loved," she'd tell us. "Now it's my job to take care of you all."

I went to high school in the outskirts of Dayton. A country school. I was a B student. My senior year I had two or three classes, then I'd go to Wright State to take college courses.

Szmauz: I come from a loving family in the mountains of southern New Hampshire. New Ipswich. It's a town of less than 5,000 people.

New Ipswich is incredibly beautiful. There's a lot of trees. It's boggy like *The Lord of the Rings*. We live on Bear Mountain. My parents have twelve acres in the middle of the woods and, growing up, I had a trail to my best friend's house.

My mom mostly stayed at home and is an artist. My dad's a computer engineer and a musician, primarily jazz piano. He got me into music when I was young.

I was rebellious. I became political at a young age. I got into Communism when I was eleven and realized that was kind of trite because it still has to do with the concept of money. I got into Marxism and finally made the transition to anarchism when I was around thirteen.

Toward the beginning of high school, I was an A student. I was in honors and AP classes till I decided that the American education system was failing and I stopped trying. I got kicked out of public school for hiding in the bathroom with a fire extinguisher and spraying people when they walked in. I went to a Catholic school and got kicked out because I have a huge problem with organized religion, and I was very vocal about it. I finally ended up at this parochial school, where I graduated early with a 3.5 GPA.

David, 62, from Harlem, New York, served in the Air Force for ten years before becoming addicted to crack and moving to Las Vegas: I grew up in the sixties and my mother and stepfather were heroin addicts and my stepfather sold heroin and cocaine. We always had company when I was growing up and I was the oldest kid, so when my mother and father were getting high I would take my sister and stepbrother to another room and we'd play in there. I'd make sure they didn't come out.

I potty-trained my sister. That's how close we were.

My stepdad was a sharp dresser and he played in a lot of sidewalk craps games. He made enemies in the street because he was a dope fiend. He'd get a package and turn it over to somebody, then the next time he would use the dope or mess up the money in some kinda way. There were times when the cops swept everybody on the avenue and he had to throw away the sack or money or both.

One time he gave me money and told me to walk to my grandmother's, which was three blocks away. I had my stepbrother and little cousin with me, and some guy robbed me in the park. I had shorts on and he saw the knot in my sock. He said, "What's that, kid?" And he grabbed me. My brother and cousin tried to stop him, but he just laughed. I wasn't old enough to do nothing about it either.

You ever hear of Charlotte Street in the Bronx? It was infamous for its abandoned buildings that were set on fire by homeless people or owners trying to collect insurance. That's where my family ended up staying. We lived four stories up, and one winter our pipes froze and we had to go to the fire hydrant to get water. The next day my grandfather came down from Otisville and got me and my sister. Took us back there, where I finished high school. I graduated in '72. There were sixteen students in my class and I was one of the top two or three.

One Shoe Sue, 51, lived in the drains for three years, like her son Shaggy. She was once arrested while wearing a single flip-flop, hence her street name: Both my parents wore uniforms. My mother was a nurse, my father was a doctor in the Navy. Our house was happy. I had three

ONE SHOE SUE

brothers and two sisters—I'm the youngest—and we did chores every Saturday. We'd go outside and play until the streetlights came on. We'd go fishing. We'd climb water towers and experiment with cigarettes. When my dad was stationed in Cuba we'd go sailing and horseback riding.

My family moved to Las Vegas in 1983, the summer before my senior year. The house we bought was abandoned and we fixed it up that summer: painted it, took out the wrought iron, cleaned the pool. My dad retired here and my mom was a little under a year sober, and everybody was looking at her sideways wondering if she was going to drink.

That summer I got into a motorcycle accident and ripped up my face. I was working at Safeway as a bag girl. I asked my mom if I could go on a motorcycle ride with a guy from work and she said no. I went anyway. He wrecked going sixty miles per hour and I didn't have a protective shield on my helmet. Flight for Life picked us up and I was flown to Valley Hospital.

After the accident I was on crutches. I broke a few ribs and was bruised terribly. I didn't go to school for the first half of the year. I stayed at home and one my friends brought me the assignments. When I went to school the movie *Scarface* had come out, so the students nicknamed me that. I didn't graduate that spring, but I went to summer school and got my diploma.

Stephen: I'm the youngest of six kids. When my mother was dropped off in Las Vegas she was eight months pregnant with me.

I grew up on the corner of Boulder Highway and Flamingo, where Sam's Town casino is now. Back then there was nothing there.

My dad was a traveling salesman. He came out here to try to get some property and become another Howard Hughes, but he couldn't stay in one place.

He left when I was two and my mother met another man. He must've been crazy to take on a woman who had six kids.

He'd put his hands on her. She finally said the hell with that and raised us in one trailer after another, then in a three-bedroom home near Tropicana and Nellis.

She worked as a cashier and was good with money. Too proud to go on welfare. She'd use coupons and go to four or five different stores. I never knew we were poor till I was older.

I don't remember seeing my mom drunk, but she used to keep a bottle of apricot brandy under the seat of the car. A couple of times I took it out and tasted it. It was hot, sweet. It burned my mouth. I was ten or eleven and it didn't bother me or do nothing for me.

Every summer my mother wanted me to be around a man because I had four sisters. My father would travel, selling whitewall tires, and we'd drive up and down the Mississippi River. I'd pull tires off cars and he'd put whitewalls on 'em. The next day we'd be in a different car lot in a different town doing the same thing.

One time on the Fourth of July we had a picnic, and we were catching frogs in the river, and there was a six-pack in the cooler. My dad didn't drink much. He'd have a beer when he had fried oysters. That was the only time I saw him drink. I was twelve or thirteen, and I was back at the hotel and he was gone, and I cracked one of the beers and ended up drinking four or five of them. All of a sudden I was running around the room screaming, "Man, this is great!"

When I was fifteen or sixteen I ended up getting a job at the International casino, just off the Strip. Now it's the Westgate. I bussed tables there.

On my breaks I'd go to the roof of the hotel. I hear a lot of people say they were born an alcoholic. I don't know about that, but I do know I was afraid from an early age. I wasn't smart. I wasn't cool and tough. So I'd act like I was, when deep inside I was scared to death.

Me and my work friends would meet on the roof and look out at the lights of the Strip and, sure enough, one of them would say, "I got a fat one. Let's smoke it."

I found out then that there were things I could smoke, drink, shoot, sniff, and pop that could take me away from that edge. I was worried that I didn't belong, but I could take a drink or a puff and everything was okay.

Zero: I don't talk about my childhood. My life was created by me. My childhood had nothing to do with who I am today.

Four Finger Mike: I was born at Nellis Air Force Base. My dad was in the Air Force for thirty years. Armaments and airplanes—that's what he knew. My mom and dad were both Depression babies. They never threw away anything. My mom said it was because when they were young they never had nothing. They wouldn't even throw away a piece of wood. Said they might need it later.

I was in the seventh grade. Woodshop class. At the time they'd have us run the wood through the saw machine and hold it down with our hand, and after it kicked out the wood my hand went down. Blood everywhere. I don't remember much else. Just the hospital. The funny thing was my mom was teaching at Clark High and it was "Hillbilly Day" or something like that, and she came to the hospital in some god-awful outfit.

They couldn't do anything to save the fingers. The machine grinded them up like sawdust. There was nothing to save. It was my left hand. The top half of the three middle fingers and the tip of the pinkie.

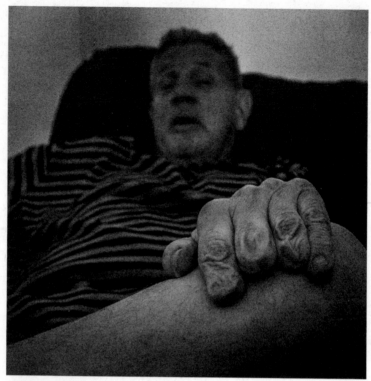

FOUR FINGER MIKE

I was ahead at Valley High and only taking one class, so I went to work at a lawyer's office as a runner. I went to school at six a.m. and to work at nine. I worked full time. The lawyer was Bill Coulthard. He was an ex-FBI agent and part-owner of the land Binion's Horseshoe casino was on.

We were going down the elevator together one Friday afternoon and he asked me if I wanted to weed his lawn tomorrow and make some extra money.

"Sure," I said.

We got off the elevator and went our separate ways, and all of a sudden a big explosion shook the parking garage. Somebody put a bomb in his car. I was the last person to see him alive. They never did discover who did it. They don't know if it was because of the Mob or Binion's or something else from his time as an FBI agent.

Pretty Boy Steve, 50, lived in the tunnels off and on for twelve years, several of those with his girlfriend Kat. A longtime front-desk clerk, he followed his father into the resort industry: We moved from California to Vegas when I was five, and I had a great childhood. We were pretty wealthy. My dad was a successful casino operator, and he was around for every birthday and holiday.

My mom was a homemaker. Once my father succeeded in the casino industry, she didn't need to work anymore and he didn't want her to. He was old-fashioned. She stayed at home and took care of us. Dinner at six. Be there or get your ass whooped.

I wasn't the greatest student. Between junior high and high school I went from a public school to a private one and I didn't like the transition. I was looking forward to going to a public school, the same one my brothers went to, but my parents didn't want me to turn out like my brothers.

I rebelled when I got to the private school. It was so much harder, a big jump. I couldn't keep up, so I cheated. By my senior year that was my curriculum: Cheating 101.

It was stressful toward the end of high school. I didn't know if I was going to graduate. I'll never forget my American government class. We had a whole unit on taxes. It might as well have been geometry or algebra. I didn't get it at all and I squeaked by with a D-. If I would've failed I wouldn't have graduated. I think they did me a favor just to get rid of me.

Ned: When I was six my dad tried to kidnap me. I was on the porch at my grandmother's house, and he pulled up and had his door open and walked up to me. I recognized him. He scooped me up and walked toward his vehicle and tried to put me in it. I kicked him where it counts, and he dropped me and I took off and ran back inside and locked the door. Haven't seen him since.

My mother emigrated from Poland. I'm first generation American. I was born and raised in Chicago on the Southside. It was pretty rough. Luckily my family endured and my mom was able to place me in a private Catholic school, Our Lady of the Snows. We had to wear uniforms, and nuns taught us. I was an altar boy.

I was touched by a priest. It never got to skin on skin, but I ended up reporting him and it was a big controversy at the school. I was in second grade. I told my mom about it and she brought it to the board, and a bunch of parents asked their sons about the situation, and the priest was put on sabbatical. I stopped having faith in the church after that.

Being an altar boy you have changing rooms. The priest would creep up behind us. I witnessed it happen to a few other boys and I'd just leave, change real fast and go.

Altar boys have to put on a smock, and one time I didn't know he was there and he crept up behind me and helped me take off my outfit, and he started to get aggressive. I broke away and ran.

The church sent in investigators. The FBI was also involved because several other reports were filed. He was taken out of our parish and sent somewhere else. I don't know what became of him.

Jamie, 53, is an accomplished guitarist and raconteur from the Deep South: I went to first grade in Louisiana. The rest of my school years were in Mississippi. I grew up in Vicksburg. My parents had seven kids, all boys. I'm the youngest, the little man. We grow 'em big in my family.

My dad was an old-school kinda guy. He was president of the Mississippi Teamsters. An honest man. Strict. No bullshit. A hardcore country-bluegrass guy. Played fifteen different instruments. He wasn't accomplished at any of them, but that's who I got my love of music from.

Mom was a housewife and she progressively lost her hearing till it was gone. You wouldn't know it if you were looking at her when you were talking. She could read lips. But her being deaf allowed me to crank my Marshall up and play as loud as I wanted to.

My high school had a designated smoking area, if that tells you anything. It was your typical small-town high school. Warren Central in Vicksburg, Mississippi.

We had an asshole principal. The guy jacked me up one day because I didn't have my shirt tucked in. He grabbed me by the arm and said, "Come into my office right now!"

We went to his office and he said, "You're suspended till your parents come here for a conference."

I started laughing. "Dude, there ain't no way my dad's gonna come down here."

He called my dad that night and my dad said, "I've been out of school for thirty years. I'm not coming there. Jamie's old enough to make his own decision, so whatever he decides it's up to him."

My dad hung up the phone and told me, "Drop out of school if you wanna. I wouldn't advise it, but if that's what you wanna do, go ahead. But your ass is getting a job. You ain't gonna just lay 'round here."

So I dropped out in tenth grade and got a job bagging groceries. I also started selling weed. That's mostly what I ended up doing: selling pot and playing music.

Melinda: I used to play with the money my mom made and dress up and act like a cocktail waitress. I'd also watch TV quietly in the dark, because it had to be dark and quiet while she slept. I'd play with my dolls in the dark.

Vegas Dee: I was shy and quiet. I stayed to myself. We were allowed to have church friends, but not secular ones.

I only went to school till tenth grade. That was in Saks, Alabama. I couldn't take it anymore because I had choke marks on my neck and I was asked what happened. I told the principal and he immediately called my dad, but nothing came of it.

My brother ended up finding some really horrible pictures my dad had taken of me tied up and stuff. He called my mom and things transpired from there. My mom stood up in front of the whole church and told everybody what happened. I was made fun of in school. That's when my rebellion kicked in. I did end up going to prom with a guy who's now in the DEA, but things went south from there.

My mom moved to Oklahoma and I followed her there. She didn't have an education, so I ended up having to work to help support the family. I worked at a place called Jalopy's, a restaurant in Perkins, right outside of Stillwater. I was a waitress. I'd just turned sixteen.

Shortly after that I met the preacher's son and ended up getting pregnant. I married him because our parents said we had to. We divorced less than a year later.

Shaggy: I got into the performing arts school, the Las Vegas Academy, as a theater major. They took me in and protected me. School was always an escape for me. I never dreaded it. I looked forward to it because I always got to get away from where I was living or who I was living with. It was the only constant in my life.

At the Academy you'd do theater every day for an hour and a half, and I threw myself into it. I wrote and produced my own show and they let me perform it, and now they have a student-performed and -directed show every year. I was the first to do it.

My favorite show was *The Laramie Project*. I played Russell Henderson, one of the guys who murdered Matthew Shepard. That was the role I dove into the most as far as character development and research. I really locked into it.

The show was originally scheduled to run for five nights, and we did it for fifteen and in front of an audience from Laramie. That was an honor.

Becky: The first time I did meth I felt like I could do anything. I was on cloud nine. It was me and my girlfriends in the city park in Lancaster, California. We went into the bathroom and snorted it. I was fifteen.

I always told myself I wouldn't do meth 'cause I'd seen what it did to my mom, but I followed her lead.

Iron, 50, lived in the drains for eight years. Raised in Oklahoma, he sought solace in drugs following a tragedy that occurred when he was in high school: The partying didn't really start till my sophomore year. This girl I was seeing, Sherrie, was coming over to say hey, and some friends that had been quail hunting gave her a ride. As one of 'em got out the back of the truck the shotgun went off and killed Sherrie. It was an accident, but it was a turning point in my life. I started experimenting with things other than alcohol.

Easy E: I was so anti-drugs. The first time I smoked weed I was fourteen and I feel asleep for several hours. When I woke up my arm was numb. I thought, Oh my God! The marijuana paralyzed my arm! I said I'd never smoke that shit again.

I graduated sixty-sixth out of sixty-nine people in my class. I'm intelligent, but not when it comes to books. I got street smarts. I didn't need math and I sure didn't need science to know how to mix chemicals, because I learned that later through my meth addiction.

I was ADD. In class I just stared off into space.

"What's the answer, Eric?"

"Fourteen?"

It was a spelling question.

I couldn't pay attention to nothing. I think I was bipolar too. I was happy-go-lucky one minute and depressed the next.

Ricky Lee: When I was fifteen or sixteen, I started living in group homes and boys' homes and youth facilities. I finished high school because I was in a prison for young people. I got most of my credits there. It was rougher than an adult prison. You got off the bus fighting or you were considered a punk. You didn't want to get punked because you'd get treated like shit the rest of the time you were there. I fought every day.

Tex: Mamma worked in factories until she went to college and got her associate degree in accounting. When I was in high school in North Carolina I used to help her with her homework. She'd get so mad at me. "Boy, you're smart, but you just won't apply yourself!" Around that time, I decided I wanted to be a pilot or a veterinarian. I went from making Fs to As.

In junior high I was in band. I played the trumpet, tuba, baritone, and French horn. I could've went somewhere with it, but you don't get girls in band. I wanted to play football and be popular.

I was pretty good at football. Turned down a scholarship and went into the Army. My future was bright.

ADULTHOOD

Jamie: I played in band after band. Blues, country, rock, metal—you name it. I was in one blues band where I was the only white guy in it. There were songs that we played that didn't even have a title. Just twelve-bar heat. Really accomplished players. Vicksburg is a hotbed of bad-ass musicians.

My metal band Malice played the very first Riverfest in 1987. We dressed like metalheads back then. I had on zebra-striped jeans, a bandana. We were good. We played Maiden and Queensrÿche and we opened that show with Ozzy's "Bark at the Moon." We knocked Vicksburg on its ass, man! They were used to hearing Elvis covers and stuff like that. There was 8,000 people there.

My family was pretty tight till our parents died. My mother was the thread that held the family together. She passed in 2004.

My dad died suddenly of an aneurysm in '96. I got a call one day saying, "Daddy's in the hospital." By the time I got there he was already on a respirator. He had two aneurysms burst at the same time. Normally one of them will kill you in five minutes; you bleed out. He lived for twelve hours, which allowed me and my brothers to see him and say, "I love you." That was the first and last time I said that to my dad.

When he died I went on a soul-searching quest. I'd sat there and watched my dad—the rock I never saw any fear or weakness in—on that bed with a tube down his throat, and he's squeezing my hand and telling me, "I can't breathe!"

That was the worst day of my life.

Knyck, 31, lived in the drains for four years and met his girlfriend Maddie there. He was born and raised in Las Vegas and graduated from Chaparral High: I went to College of Southern Nevada. That was the first time I took school seriously. High school was just bullshit to me, but I loved college. I felt like I was really educating myself. I could choose the classes I wanted and I took a full load. Anthropology and sociology and a bunch of other interesting classes, and I aced them all.

One Shoe Sue: My dad didn't speak to me for a year after the motorcycle accident, and I was supposed to go to college, but that changed. He had money saved for college; it went into my face instead. He bought me a little beater car and I went on with my life.

I moved to California with some girlfriends and got a job as a phone operator. We lived in Anaheim right by Disneyland. We could see the fireworks every night from our balcony. But I met this guy and the first time I slept with him I got pregnant, and within a couple months I was calling my mom and wanting to come home to Vegas. I came home four months pregnant in my Mustang with a U-Haul trailer hitched to the back.

The baby's father sent me ahead. I should've known that something was wrong. We had been doing speed together, but I didn't realize the amount he was doing. We got married and I had the baby, and we were living in an apartment up the street from my parents. I came home one day and he was snorting speed. I moved in with my parents and he went to Florida, and I never saw him again. He left when our son, Shaggy, was two years old.

After Shaggy's father left, I got married again. The guy said I had to get rid of the kid, so I gave him to my family when he was seven or eight. I eventually divorced that guy, but I couldn't see my son because I couldn't stay sober—I was drinking and smoking crack—and my parents were disgusted with me.

I'd smoked crack before, but I wasn't really down with it, then someone threw a pipe in front of me and taught me how to smoke it and it was a wrap. It was a girl who wanted to turn me out—you know, show me how to prostitute.

We'd go into grocery stores and steal and I'd be so scared. She'd put bottles of alcohol into her pocket or just run with them. There were a few girls like that—real renegades—on the streets. They'd teach you how to survive, get you in trouble, then disappear. That happened to me a lot with women. I never worked for a man.

Ricky Lee: I didn't have any plans. I never made plans. I lived day to day. Because I'd read so many books I wanted to be free, like the characters in them, but I ended up going to prison a lot.

Plato. Milton. Edgar Allan Poe. I can't remember all my favorite authors off the top of my head, but I like poets. I like philosophers too.

RICKY LEE

Books take me to a different time and I live in it when I read them. I relate to the characters and live their lives instead of mine.

I never did drugs till I was in my late twenties, but I started going to prison as a teenager and that continued when I was an adult. From '84 to '92 I spent only three months out of prison. I liked prison. It was cool. All my friends were there. No one left. You got out on vacation and then you came back.

I did all my probation in prison. That was my choice.

Tex: I was serving in the Military Police in Panama when I found out my mom died. The coroner's report said her death was undetermined, but I believe my stepdad had something to do with it and I felt like I wasn't there to protect her. After that my world started going down the tubes. She was everything to me. I stayed in the military and went to Desert Storm in '91 and got hit by an RPG and lost hearing in my left ear and almost lost my leg.

When my time was up, I left the military. I should've stayed in, but my wife told me she couldn't handle somebody knocking on her door and telling her, "We're sorry to inform you that your husband was KIA." She said it was either the military or her and the kids, and I went back to North Carolina to be with them.

My wife's stepdad Pat was crazy. He'd just gotten another DUI and my wife's mother had kicked him out and he needed a place to live before he went to prison and he was staying with us. He was violent and I was scared of him.

The boiling point came when I heard my daughter screaming. She was two years old. I go into the living room and Pat had her by the arm and he's beating her with a hardback edition of Stephen King's *The Stand*. That's the book he was reading and he was whooping her for cutting the light on and off.

I said, "Don't ever discipline my daughter! Get your shit and get outta my house and don't ever come back!"

He went to a payphone and called my wife's mom and she was coming to pick him up. He was standing at the door and he said, "You know I'm gonna have to get you now," and he pulled out a knife.

I'm sitting on the couch and my gun cabinet is cattycorner to me. I had a .45 and .380 and I kept the .380 locked and loaded with the safety on. I reached down, jerked the cabinet open, pulled out the pistol, and stood up, and he took two and a half steps toward me. When I seen that braided blade, I shot him three times.

TEX

They said if I'd shot him once or six times they wouldn't have charged me. Once would've shown I was just trying to stop him and six would've shown I was temporarily insane, but because I stopped after three I was in my right mind and I used excessive force.

In the military they train you to shoot in three-round bursts. Boom, boom, boom! If your target's not down you re-center on it and fire three more times, 'cause you can't carry a lot of ammo in the field and you gotta make it last. My target was down after three shots so I stopped firing.

They charged me with first-degree murder with malice and forethought. I had an 85 percent chance of being acquitted and a 15 percent chance of spending the rest of my life in prison. When they come to me with manslaughter I pled guilty and got five years.

Iron: My daughter Ashli was born in November 1989. Her mother and I never got married. We broke up because I was drinking, smoking weed, and doing dope. You've heard the saying, "Instant asshole. Just add alcohol." That was me. You give me a bottle of tequila and there's gonna be a fight.

I went through a time when I dealt with everything with my fists. I hurt a lot of people and I chose to remove myself from my daughter and her mom's lives. I felt I was making the right decision by distancing myself from them, but maybe I was just trying to make myself feel better about everything that had happened. Maybe I was removing myself from a bad situation that I helped create.

Merch: I went to Bowling Green for two years and left to work for General Motors. I worked in a big room on the third floor. There was a chain basket that ran through a tunnel, and I would take boxes off it and stack them. I was supplying the assembly line with parts.

I enjoyed it. It was an easy job. I worked two or three hours a day, then I just waited for trucks to come and I'd help unload them.

Sweeny, 48, was born and raised in the Pacific Northwest. After graduating from high school, he attended Portland State for a few semesters, then enlisted in the Marine Corps. He lived in the drains with a small community that included Pretty Boy Steve, Kat, Phil, Easy E, Manny, and Melinda: I originally signed up to go infantry, which is the basic Marine Corps job. Ended up going to boot camp in San Diego for three months. It was tough. Real physical. Being yelled at is the main thing. They tear you down before they build you up.

The first month they give you a test because they're looking for linguists. I did well on the test, so that gave me the opportunity to move to the signals-intelligence field, which was basically listening to traffic in the Russian language. In the late eighties and early nineties they were still the enemy. There were about ten posts around the world where you dealt with that traffic. Working in a building with these huge round antennas, intercepting signals, and analyzing them for the Marine Corps and NSA.

Linguist training is in Monterey, California. I spent a year there learning Russian, then I went to San Angelo, Texas, to learn the military side of things. After that I spent two years in Guam and two in Scotland.

I enjoyed it. Our units were small and we worked well together. When we weren't working we were drinking. That's when the partying started for me. We worked for three days, then had three off. The alcohol on base was cheap, especially in Guam, and there were a lot of Navy chicks there. Those three days off we were partying or doing physical training, which you learn to do hungover or still drunk. We thought that was part of being a Marine.

Szmauz: I started landscaping and was in a band. I play a lot of instruments, but in that particular band, Brave Ulysses, I was lead guitarist and lead singer. We were pretty good. We won the New England Battle of the Bands and got offered free recording time at a studio, but my addiction was progressing rapidly because I immersed myself in that mindset of sex, drugs, and rock 'n' roll. My biggest influences were Kurt Cobain, Syd Barrett, Sid Vicious, and Jim Morrison. My goal was to join the Twenty-Seven Club—to die at the age of twenty-seven—like so many great musicians.

We were playing a music festival and the whole band ate a bunch of mushrooms. The keyboardist was freaking out because he thought the keyboard was out of tune. Our drummer kept telling me the kit was on fire and blindingly red. I played the entire set lying down on the stage. It was at night and I was looking at the stars, losing my mind.

Phil: February 1990. I was staying at my mom and dad's house in Mira Loma, California. Richelle, my wife at the time, was upstairs with my oldest daughter Jessica. I woke up and went downstairs to see what was going on. My dad was sitting in the living room and this guy was hooking up some Venetian blinds.

My father told me, "We just ran outta milk. Go to the store and get some."

When I got back the garage door was open and one of our dogs was running around the worker's van. I'm like, What the hell?

These were bad times and I was a bad guy. I kept a gun underneath my seat, but I didn't bring it in the house this time. Usually I'd have it tucked in my waistband and I'd walk upstairs and put it in the closet.

I came inside and the blinds guy was on top of my father, driving him into the concrete floor. Blood was coming out of my dad's nose. My reaction was to hit the guy and get him off my dad, until I realized how big this motherfucker was. There wasn't a damn thing my skinny ass could do.

I was screaming for my brother. He's been in martial arts ever since he was a kid and he's a fifth-degree black belt. He came and jumped over the railing and the guy ran. As I got to my car and grabbed the gun, my brother got in the way and my wife was screaming, "Phil, no!"

The guy jumped in the van and I started shooting, but I didn't hit him and he drove off. I chased him, but couldn't find him.

I got back home and my dad was still on the living-room floor. Me and my brother helped him get to his bedroom. He must've known he was dying. He had a heart attack during the fight and he regurgitated the Frosted Flakes he had for breakfast and they went into his lungs and filled them completely. It's like diving into the ocean and you can't make it to the surface.

In his deposition the blinds guy told his story. He was over 300 pounds. He played football for San Diego State. A lineman. This was his summer job. He worked for a drapery company that was contracted by Sears. He said that my dad went after him, that a fight broke out in the house. That's not my dad. My dad was an ex-cop.

The guy never had any charges brought against him because in California a homicide has to meet five criteria, and they said it didn't meet any of them. He got off completely.

My mother sued the drapery company and Sears for wrongful death and she got some money, but no money could bring back my pops. To make matters worse the dumbasses took me to jail for discharging a weapon in the city limits.

The whole thing made me mad about the law and how life works. You can take someone's life and the dead man can't tell no tales. That made me step across the threshold even further with guns and drugs.

Four Finger Mike: I went to UNLV. Got into a fraternity. Had a frat house with a pool. It was like *Animal House*. That's the best way to describe it.

I didn't graduate. Ended up working the front desk at the Marina Hotel. I was nineteen years old. I worked one day shift, two swings, and two graves. The day I turned twenty-one I learned how to deal cards and a month later they hired me as a dealer. This was 1976 and I made $100 a day. Bye-bye college, hello drugs.

There was a small hotel across from the Tropicana that had a downstairs bar called the Nineteenth Hole. Ruben was the bartender and people would be doing lines of coke off the bar while hookers were giving them blowjobs. I fell right into that lifestyle.

Right around when UNLV won the men's basketball championship, I had money in the bank and I was running the Marina's race and sportsbook. I don't want to implicate myself, but we were making a lot of money. On the weekend I was coming home with $1,000 extra, and it was all going to cocaine and prostitutes.

One night I was in bed with two girls in a townhouse I owned and they said, "Why don't we try some of this? We can get freakier if we're on it." We smoked some crack and I loved it. It was euphoric.

Within two years I was outta money. I started hustling hard, stealing money to get crack. I was a bucket thief on the Strip. Other thieves would throw money on the floor, and when the person turned to pick it up they'd grab their coin bucket and run. I'd just move a divider between slot machines and slide their bucket to my side and walk away.

Shaggy: I was in a downward spiral. I'd already burned most of the bridges with my family. I was so upset with them and the way things had gone. It got to the point where they didn't want to tell me what was going on with my mother because it was all bad.

I was living in a place we dubbed the "Clown House." We called it that because I juggled for a short period of time. Seven or eight of us lived there together from the age of seventeen to twenty. It started with a core group from the Las Vegas Academy and spread from there. It was communal—and complete and utter chaos. I started doing heroin there. A girl I knew introduced me to it. At first it didn't take, but eventually it got a hold on me.

Half Pint: One of my brothers had a learning disability, and they didn't have special ed in western Nebraska when he was growing up. I watched my parents struggle with that. The anguish in my mom's eyes. That led me to special education.

I left Drury College with a teaching degree and was certified in Nebraska, Missouri, Kansas, and Texas.

David: It happened at a sidewalk craps game. As I understand it there was an argument over fifty cents, and a guy who was an enemy of my stepfather pulled out a pistol and shot him twice in the chest and killed him. My dad was forty at the time and I was nineteen, but we'd just started getting close. I hated him as a kid, but as an adult we bonded.

After my stepfather got killed I started thinking about my life. I was hanging out at this rough, bucket-of-blood bar. There was fights every night. I didn't have a hustle. I was searching for something to do and my uncle Nick, who I loved dearly, said I should join the Air Force.

My first station was in Louisiana. Barksdale Air Force Base. That's where I met my baby momma. She was working on base and I was looking for a girl, so me and her started messing around. Then I got assigned to England.

Black men get all kinds of rhythm in England. It's unbelievable. I could write a book about my experience with English girls. They preferred black men. White guys couldn't even get a dance. I'm in that atmosphere, but also missing my girl. We were keeping in touch by letters and cassette tapes. I'm playing music on the tapes and talking over it to her. I felt if she could hear my voice I could hang onto her.

After six months in England I went back to Louisiana on leave and married her. She'd told me she was pregnant. She wasn't. She had three kids when I met her and I told her if I got her pregnant I would stick by her. When I came home on leave to marry her I noticed she wasn't big. She gave me some story about a miscarriage, but I was in love with her, so we got married anyway and she and the kids came to England with me.

Ande: For some strange reason my dad wouldn't pay for my college, even though he had more money than Midas. I couldn't get a scholarship because of his income, so I went to an outdoor school and worked as a cabin leader, and that's where I met my first two loves.

Lynn and I were together about three years. Marge was a teacher there, and she hated me at first and then, all of sudden, she fell in love with me too. I had two women I was balancing. I hiked into Yosemite and asked God which one should I choose.

He said, "Neither."

"Why?" I asked Him.

"You're going to be alone for most of your life."

So I set them both free.

I don't give a damn if anyone believes me. When I was in my mid-twenties I had a conversation with God over a three-month span and He told me my entire life: who I was going to meet, who I needed to help, what I was going to do, and what I was going to go through. He told me I was going to live in a tunnel.

ANDE

I said, "Why?"

And He said, "Because you need to learn to appreciate what you have."

After the outdoor school I was working at my dad's factory on the assembly line—he was an executive for Xerox—and I got my associate degree at Fullerton Junior College. I popped over to Cal State and finished my bachelor's in psychology with a minor in business. Thought about going for an MBA, but statistics bugged me, and those people dress weird and are stuffy. I wanted to do something with business and psychology, and I found out that Long Beach State had a program like that, so I went there for my master's. Then I got my PhD in organizational behavior and human factors from Claremont Graduate University in '99.

When I was in grad school I was working at McDonnell Douglas and I kept getting promoted. At one point I was the manufacturing coordinator, working in the department where all the parts were made. One of the satellites we made was for the Star Wars program, so I got to shake Dan Quayle's hand and get recognized by the White House. Another satellite helped bring cable TV to Great Britain, so Margaret Thatcher called and thanked us.

At thirty-four I stopped and looked around. I was making $60,000 a year. I was a single woman and my rent in Long Beach was only $650 a month. I had a cute apartment. French windows. My front door was in a turret. I was happy.

I was also going for astronaut candidacy. McDonnell Douglas had sent one of their employees into space, and research was being done on astronauts going crazy and becoming suicidal. I wanted to be the first shrink in space. I wanted to be up there to help the astronauts if they needed it. That was my obsession.

But as I kept getting older I realized that a PhD might not be enough to get me into space. Then the Challenger blew up and they did away with payload specialists—extra people who could get on board with the mission specialists. When the realization hit me, I decided to have a cigarette and a beer. That turned into a six-pack. And so on. And so on.

Barry: I got accused of molesting my cousins, two boys under the age of ten. Had a public defender who was more interested in getting a plea deal than proving me innocent. I was forced to plead guilty to a crime I didn't commit and spend eighteen years, three months, and ten days in prison.

It was the boys' words against mine, and I was a repeat offender. In a case like that if you don't have proof you didn't do it, you're presumed guilty.

Vegas Dee: I ended up moving to Atlanta with my kids and starting a website. It was an adult site. It wasn't porn. You couldn't see any sex. You'd just see a gallery and you'd pick a girl. Guys would pay per minute to spend time with them online. I found the girls through Cheetah and Pink Pony strip clubs. I was on the radio. I had a billboard. My content was amazing and I was making good money.

That's when I started breaking into the darker side of the world. It was intriguing to me because I'd come from a strict, religious background, and I thought maybe I'd find the answer to why my dad did what he did.

I didn't like Ned when I met him. Didn't pay him any mind. I was young and super cute, and I had started using and dealing drugs.

I met him through a friend I dealt to. There was a party one night and Ned was there. He kept asking my friend, "Who's that girl?"

I hung out with him that night and he seemed pretty cool and sociable, and two days later he called me and said, "I'm headed to Valdosta and was wondering if I could get something." He wanted a hundred ecstasy pills.

"Yeah, I can swing that." I was moving over a thousand pills a day.

I remember seeing the Atlanta skyline in the rearview mirror. At the time I thought, This kid has no idea what I do. I'm going to ruin him.

We popped some pills, went down to South Georgia, then came back, and I didn't call him for a while. He called me and I went over to his house. He had a penthouse in Buckhead. I'd lost my house, kids, everything because of arrests and drug use. I said, "I'll come live with you." But I warned him, "I deal with some really bad people."

He went into his bedroom and came out guns blazing. He had Glock 9s and .22-calibers. I thought, Okay. This guy can hang.

But he failed to tell me he was delinquent on three months' rent. The day after I moved in, our stuff was sitting on the side of Peachtree Street.

Ned: I ventured to Georgia. One of my cousins married into a prominent family there. Eventually I found a sales job in Tifton. Vacuums door to door. That was my first legitimate job in sales. It took me a month before anyone even let me through the door to do a presentation.

Later I got into car sales. Taylor BMW in Augusta. A guy named Alan took me under his wing and taught me how to treat clients, from the meet and greet to the sign and drive, and I became pretty well established in the industry and was offered a position in Atlanta with Hank Aaron BMW.

Dee and I were both very entrepreneurial. If we could make a quick $500 or $1,000 we'd pull a lick.

I liked the Hank Aaron BMW job, but I was partying hard and it was easy for me to make ridiculous amounts of money doing other things. I eventually started stealing cars. Got caught for it. Did some time. Obviously, you're not going to get hired back in car sales with a GTA on your record.

I was in this stolen BMW and was doing a drop for somebody in South Georgia and it was a three-hour road trip and I took Dee with me. The whole way down we were eating ecstasy pills like PEZ candy. By the time we got to our destination we were looped and she was scared because it was really backwoods. She started calling her friends, saying, "Oh my God! I don't know what this guy's gonna do to me! I don't know what I've gotten into!"

That was our first date.

Becky: I'd moved from Lancaster, California, to Utah. One of my neighbors, a pretty young thing, went to Vegas for a good time and came back with this homeless guy, Travis. They met on one of the bridges on the Strip and she even went down into the tunnels with him, where he lived at the time.

She was like, "He's homeless and cute and I can help him."

We started hanging out with Travis and one day he was talking on the phone to his friend Zero. I started talking to Zero and we kept in touch, and eventually we figured out that we liked each other.

I'd relapsed shortly before Zero came to Utah and we fell in love so quickly and so hard that we both got addicted together. I would've done anything he asked me to and followed him anywhere.

Zero: When I was twenty-three I had a poker game at my apartment every week. We'd smoke weed and drink, and then a few of the guys decided they were comfortable bringing over coke. I wound up doing it. Man, that shit woke me up! I was feeling good and ready to go out and drink and get laid. The coke would keep me partying—and in New Orleans you have to do a lot of partying. It's required.

Crack came from that same poker group, from a good friend I grew up with. I don't blame him for it because he was addicted.

He was like, "It's just like coke, but it hits you all at once."

Actually, in some ways, drugs helped save my life. I didn't use them and get all sad. They made me feel happy and alive.

My sister was a lawyer. She was successful, but she was an alcoholic and had multiple DUIs and had her law license suspended. I worked for her awhile: filing abstracts, running documents, menial office shit. I did that for two years and also lived with her.

One night she was shitfaced and went off on me. Yelling and attacking me. I called Becky and told her I can't take this anymore. I'm moving to Vegas or Utah. I chose Utah because I wanted to meet Becky.

Pretty Boy Steve: I started at UNLV and had a girlfriend who was smart. I was Stoner Steve and she was Straight Mary. With her and her mother's help I got into UNLV, but it was the same as high school—no studying and a lot of cheating. Then she went to college in California and I was on my own. I loved UNLV. I loved the Runnin' Rebs. This was '86 to '89 and they were really good. Being a student you got free tickets, but you had to go full time, so I would sign up and then drop classes after I got my tickets.

The school started asking me what I was going to major in and it was all leading to hotel management. I got into those classes and got bored. It just didn't make sense anymore. In high school I felt like I had to graduate. At UNLV it didn't seem that way. I was wasting my parents' money and after two years I dropped out. I started working the front desk at my dad's hotel and I did that for thirteen years.

I liked the work. I answered the phones, took reservations, helped check people in. A lot of problem solving. At the desk you have to have snap answers. "Where's the Stardust?" "Do you have any rooms Friday night?" "What show should we see?"

It helped develop the leadership skills I used on the streets and in the tunnels.

SIN CITY

Fall 1997. Atlanta, Georgia. A few aimless years after graduating from college, I was paying my dues as a writer: reading "the classics" at night, working on (very amateurish) short stories and novels in the morning, and delivering the *Atlanta Journal* in the afternoon.

The paper route, though hard on my beat-up Honda Civic and my self-confidence, was easy money. It wound through the dogwood-lined suburbs of the city and I could've delivered it blindfolded. But I didn't want to become stuck, like some carriers at the warehouse, with nowhere to go except the next address, nothing to look forward to but the weekend (when the *Journal* wasn't delivered). Furthermore, my first love and I had broken up and I was playing bar trivia five days a week. I needed a change. So I turned in my route book, loaded the Civic with my worldly possessions, and moved to Las Vegas.

It seemed to make sense at the time. Judging from the books *Literary Las Vegas* and *Fear and Loathing in Las Vegas* (I'd never visited the city and didn't know anyone there), it was an intriguing place to set short stories and novels. I could sports-bet without having to call a toll-free number in the Caribbean. I wanted to explore the West and Southwest.

I planned to stay in Vegas for a year or two. I stayed twenty.

I thought my story about how I ended up in Las Vegas was interesting and unique, but it's fairly typical. I've met few Las Vegans who moved there for a job, to go to school, or for warmer weather. The reason was usually more convoluted than that—and never boring. It was equal parts running away from something and running to something, and that something was often shady, if not downright dark.

"How did you end up in Vegas?" A simple question that usually yields a complicated answer.

Tommy, 61, is a recovering alcoholic who lived in the tunnels for five years. The youngest of sixteen children, he grew up in Denver. After graduating from high school, he served in the Army and then worked construction in Colorado and California: I got into a high-speed chase in California. I was living in Riverside and had a pound of weed on me. Was using and selling it. I was speeding, so the cops came to pull me over on my motorcycle, a Honda v65, which was really fast.

I ran because of the weed. It was in my backpack. I took the backpack off and put it between my legs and was flying down the 91, crumbling weed in my hand and dropping it to the ground. When I got rid of all the evidence I pulled over.

The cop said, "What the hell, man?"

I said, "Just thought I'd take it for a ride. See what it could do."

"It looked like you were trying to get rid of something."

"I wasn't trying to get rid of anything, man."

I was put in the county jail for the high-speed chase. Did a year and after I got out I was on probation for another year. The day I got off probation I split. I said I'm done with this place and I came to Las Vegas. It was something different, a party place. I'd heard you could drink 24/7 and that sounded good to me.

TOMMY

Barry: In prison I saw a show on TV about there being work in North Dakota. When I was released after eighteen years, I went there and was working for Labor Ready in Bismarck. I was supposed to go back to Michigan to pick up a few things. Called my dad to see if I could and he said if I showed up there I'd be shot dead on the spot. My last words to him were, "Fuck you too, Dad," and I hung up the phone. I could've gone anywhere I wanted to, but I caught a bus to Las Vegas so I could have another shot at life.

Half Pint: After teaching middle school in Texas for twenty years I was asked to leave. I couldn't show up for work because I was fucked up all the time. Denied them a drug test. They called me and said, "You're not going to get an adequate evaluation. You might want to look for work somewhere else."

This was 2002. Las Vegas was hiring then. Booming. Not only that, they were giving teachers a $5,000 signing bonus and $3,000 moving expenses, so that's where I went.

Loved it! Alcohol served 'round the clock and a big enough school district that you could screw up and move schools every year, and they didn't care. And that's exactly what I did, along with some gambling. You don't make much money teaching, so I went out and tried to make a little more.

Szmauz: I went to San Diego to go to rehab, to get away from my New Hampshire environment and the music and drug scene, and the center kicked me out, so I was homeless there bouncing back and forth between Mexico. I got hooked up with a guy who ran a pharmacy in Tijuana. He'd give me a half-ounce of heroin for twenty bucks, and I'd put it in my butt and come back to San Diego and sell a gram for sixty dollars.

I reached out for help one day because I couldn't take it any more—the cartels and border crossings and homelessness and all. The addiction center in San Diego referred me to a clinic in Vegas. I completed that program and went to a sober-living home there.

I thought the city was cool at first. I'd go to the outskirts and look down on everything from the mountains. It was beautiful until I got to where the people actually lived and I was like, This place sucks! I learned real quick that Vegas will chew you up and spit you out.

The guy that was running the sober-living house kicked me out and I was homeless again and I met this guy Jordan. I'll never forget him. He was my road dog. We were breaking into houses left and right. Stealing car batteries and selling them to used battery stores. We robbed Jamba Juices. We robbed this Mexican cantina, and as we ran out the doors we looked back and twelve guys were chasing us. We booked into a park and lost them. They were older and we were younger and on meth, so they had no chance of catching us.

We lived in an abandoned building behind the Leslie's Pool Supplies near Charleston and Decatur. That's where my meth addiction increased tenfold. I was doing heroin to not be sick and meth to get high.

Jordan was thirty-two, five-foot-six, and scruffy. A ginger. If you looked into his eyes you could see he was devoid of a soul. Pure evil. He wore a trench coat and carried a sawed-off shotgun with him everywhere he went. The last time I saw him we were in the abandoned building, and I was in my area doing meth, and he comes barreling through a window and throws the gun in my lap and says, "Get rid of it!"

I'm freaking out because I'm on meth and I'm like, What the fuck?

A couple weeks prior to this I'd been complaining about a guy at an abandoned property in the neighborhood. He was the caretaker and he was hassling me for cutting through. When Jordan threw the gun in my lap he said, "You don't have to worry about that guy anymore."

I threw the gun down and booked outta there and slept behind a Burger King that night. I found out later that Jordan shot at the guy, but didn't hit him.

Sweeny: After six years in the Marine Corps I was transferred from signals-intelligence to counterintelligence. The counterintelligence school was in Dam Neck, Virginia. I went to school for five days and had two off, and on weekends we'd go out drinking in Virginia Beach. That's how I met a girl and we ended up getting married.

For the counterintelligence work I'd be gone ten months out of the year. That was hard on the marriage. That's why, at the end of my ten years, I decided not to reenlist.

My wife and I ended up in Washington state. I went there to join the police in Yakima. Did that for a year. At the end of the probationary period they didn't keep me. Nothing bad. They basically said I was too nice.

Being a cop was my dream job and I had a tough time finding another one. I got depressed and it affected the marriage. I started to drink heavily. Eventually the marriage broke up, mostly because of me and my depression and drinking. I don't have a bad thing to say about my ex.

She went back to the East Coast and I stayed in Washington looking for work. I was running out of savings. It got to the point where I realized I'd paid rent for the last month, but I wasn't sure I was going to be able to pay next month. I decided to pack my stuff and drive to Vegas. I'm still trying to figure out why. I guess I figured if I couldn't find anything else, I knew sports and I could make some money betting on it, but you know how that turns out.

Merch: My mother brought me and my sister out here as a birthday present. We came on vacation. On the third day I won.$3,000 on a slot machine at the Stratosphere and I decided that maybe I can win all the time. A month later I bought a plane ticket and moved here.

I went to the Little White Wedding Chapel and showed the owner some of my photography. Amateur work, but I'd always been passionate about it. She hired me on the spot and I was suddenly a wedding photographer. I would take couples' photos. Set 'em up. Pose 'em. It was fun and easy.

I lived next door at the Thunderbird hotel. Paid by the week. At night I'd be on call. If a couple came in the manager would call me and I'd run over and shoot the wedding.

Ricky Lee: I went through a divorce and was on the run—I was on a work furlough and never went back—and I packed a bag full of clothes and hitchhiked across the country for two years. Coast to coast. I just wanted to get away from her and everything else. Everything was coming down on me.

It all ended in Vegas. I'd stolen my ex-wife's car and fell asleep on the side of I-15 while looking at the light of the Luxor. I didn't want to give the cop my name, so I gave him my brother's. I remembered his Social Security number because it was close to mine, and gave him that too.

The cop said, "You're wanted for drunk driving."

"I don't drink!"

"You got three DUIs."

I forgot that my brother's a drinker. They booked me and found out who I was. When I was released I didn't have a car or anything, so I just stayed here.

Ned: Dee and I dipped out of Atlanta together. We packed our stuff and ended up in Glenwood Springs, Colorado, where I went to high school. I told her it was a good place for us to settle down. We got jobs. I worked in construction and she was a waitress, but our partying and hustling didn't stop. We were selling cocaine and got robbed by one of our dealers. We tried to make an investment and got $12,000 stolen from us. We tracked him down in the wee hours of the morning and broke into his room, and I started hitting people with brass knuckles. I beat up four dudes and told Dee to get our money and go, and we found the keys to their car. We ended up getting our cash back plus six ounces of cocaine and we stole their car and drove to Vegas.

Vegas Dee: Me and Ned were behind the Stardust casino. Girls Girls Girls strip club was across the street and there was an old man who sold jewelry in the area. He said, "I'll give you twenty bucks to give me a ride to the Stardust."

I said, "It's right there!"

He's like, "I'm getting in the car. Don't worry."

This guy's edgy. I like it!

He gets in the car and I tell him, "We just arrived from Colorado and don't know anything about the place. You wanna give us the rundown?"

"You just hit the jackpot, honey! You know who I am?"

"No, I don't," I said, "and frankly I don't give a shit."

"I'm Sam Angel!" The famous gambler and hustler. He was the first person we met in Vegas.

Becky: After Zero moved to Utah and started doing dope again, he got paranoid and didn't go to work one night and he's thinking he's fired. He's got no income so he might as well go to Vegas to make some money. Gambling is Zero's other addiction—the one he can't control.

He said, "Do you wanna come with me?"

My daughter was living with her dad and I thought what better time than now. We got on a Greyhound bus and came here in '09.

Zero: I didn't want to stay in Utah. I didn't like the people. I felt scrutinized by them.

Before moving to Utah, I had spent some time in Biloxi and Tunica, and this guy Bobby taught me how to survive when I didn't know what I was doing. I was a gambler. I played poker and video poker. After I played poker I'd go to the bar and get a beer or two and play the machines. Bobby saw me there and he goes, "You having any luck?"

"Not really."

"You wanna make some money instead of losing it?"

"I'm not gay, dude."

"Fuck you, man!"

"Relax. It was a joke." I was down to my last few dollars so I said, "Whatcha got?"

"I ran outta money on this Piggy Bank machine and it's ready to hit."

I didn't have anything to lose, so I put my last few dollars in the machine and boom! I hit for twenty-five dollars and then for ten. I thought, Hey, this is pretty cool.

Then he said, "This one's ready to hit too."

I played it and won more money.

We made about $300 on the Piggy Bank machines and he said, "Now I'm going to show you how to play the Odysseys."

I knew that everything Bobby had taught me in Biloxi and Tunica would come in handy in Las Vegas. I had to go there. It was my obvious next destination.

Easy E: Nothing was working out for me in New York and my dad had just got me a new car. The day the title showed up I looked down at it. My best friend had just moved to Vegas. I said, "Fuck it! I'm going there too!"

I stuffed the title into my pocket and went into my dad's room. In the top drawer was a little box; there was always a stack of hundreds in there. I took $900 and packed my shit. I grabbed the family dog and got in the car, but at the end of the street I let the dog out. If I'd taken him my dad would've found out where I was and killed me.

You remember the pocket protectors that had maps in them? They had like ten interstates on them and nothing else? I bought one of those and used the map to get all the way to Vegas in three days. I got off the 15 at Flamingo, turned on Valley View, and parked in front of Green Valley Grocery. I called my friend on the payphone and he said, "Where you at?"

"Valley View and Twain."

"Wait right there."

I go inside the store to get a pack of cigarettes and a Coke, and I come back out and he's sitting on the hood of my car. Turns out he lived right across the street.

I sold the car the next day. I owed my friend $700 and I gave him $1,000. We went out that night and I hit four deuces on a machine and I said, "I love this fucking place!"

I'd just gotten into town and I had $3,000 in my pocket.

My friend hooked me up with a place at Sierra Vista and Cambridge, and I was there two days when I ran into a twenty-year-old blonde-haired, blue-eyed goddess in a beige bikini who had a six-pack stomach. With her fifty-year-old boyfriend right behind her, she runs her hand across my cheek and under my chin and lifts my chin and says, "You're cute. What are you doing later?"

I looked at her old man and said, "Kicking his ass."

He laughed. Little did I know they were both meth addicts.

She asked me what my apartment number was and I told her. She comes over two hours later and walks in and says, "You want to do some crystal?"

"What the hell is that?" I'd never seen crack or heroin or crystal at the time.

"It's like coke, but it lasts longer."

This chick was hot and I was gonna do whatever I had to to get some of that.

She cuts me a line as big as my thumb. "Be careful," she said. "You might not wanna do all of it."

"If it's like coke I can handle it."

I run the rail and it turns out the meth was made by the Hells Angels. It's called lemon-drop dope and it smells like cat piss. When I snorted it, it felt like grabbing a red-hot poker and shoving it straight into my brain. I was ready

EASY E

to kill this chick. It took me ten minutes to even begin to handle the pain. I was covered head to toe in sweat, as if I'd been standing under the biggest, darkest cloud.

I said, "I need to take a shower." I come out fifteen minutes later. "What do you wanna do?" I'm going a thousand miles an hour. I've never been so high in my life, and I still had the $3,000. "How much does this shit cost?"

"How much do you need?" she said.

All I knew in drug terminology was an eight-ball 'cause that's how we used to buy cocaine. "How much is an eight-ball?"

"A hundred and fifty dollars."

We buy this huge rock of meth, then catch a ride to Binion's casino. It's July. I'm wearing black work boots, long black pants, a long-sleeve Raiders jersey, and my Raiders hat. The thermometer on top of Binion's read 113 degrees.

She asked me for twenty dollars, then disappeared. I go to the blackjack table. I'm so high I'm doubling down on twelves.

The dealer looks at me and says, "Sir, are you sure you want to do that?"

My eyes are bugged out and I say, "I know what I'm doing."

He turns to the pit boss and mumbles, "This guy's high as a kite, but he's the luckiest son of a bitch I've ever seen."

I was up $2,000 at one point, but at six in the morning I didn't have a dime in my pocket. The girl had my dope and my last twenty dollars and she hadn't returned.

I started walking. I had no idea where I was going. Finally I ended up at the Target on Maryland and Flamingo, but not knowing exactly where I was. My face was covered with heat sores. I'd had nothing to drink. When you're on meth your body sucks every little bit of juice out of you. It's like wringing out a sponge and setting it in the sun.

My buddy shows up and I tell him to go inside and get a pack of cigarettes and a jug of water. I weighed myself the day before and was 231 pounds. We get back to my apartment and I stepped on the scale: 200. In fourteen hours I'd lost thirty-one pounds.

I take an ice bath to try to bring my temperature down. I'm in there for thirty minutes when the bathroom door opens and that cunt walks in.

"I'm gonna kill you!" I said. "Where'd you go? Where's my dope? Where's my money?" I jump out of the water butt naked and she laughs, so now I'm even madder. I ain't well-endowed to begin with and the ice bath only made matters worse. "You bitch! You probably sold my dope, didn't you?"

"I did," she said. Then she put $300 and two bags of dope on the sink.

I got quiet. Finally I said, "Okay. That's cool." And we went right back to snorting dope.

Tex: After pleading guilty to manslaughter for shooting my wife's stepdad, I was a model prisoner for thirteen months and was released. I got home and found out my wife was sleeping around with everyone, so we got a divorce. I ended up moving to Minnesota and was dating an Ojibwe Indian. The Indians didn't like a white boy being with a native girl, and I decided it was time to get the hell outta there and go to Vegas.

I got off the bus with a hundred dollars to my name and ended up at Sahara and Las Vegas Boulevard. I was thirsty and wanted a Mountain Dew. I was gonna get my Dew and go across the street to a motel. The sign said thirty dollars a night. I was gonna get cleaned up and find a job the next day. I go into a Circle K and set the Mountain Dew on the counter and hand the clerk the $100 bill.

She said, "You have to put it in the 'validator.'"

"What the hell is a validator?"

"The machine that tells us if it's real or not."

I was used to the way things were in North Carolina and Texas—everybody left their home unlocked, their truck running to go into the store, their phone in the truck.

I walked outta the store with ninety-eight dollars and change, and all I could think about was popping that Mountain Dew. I tip it back and next thing I know, out of nowhere, this little motherfucker comes running by and jerks the cash right out of my hand. By the time the change hit the scalding asphalt he was gone.

I called the cops and they said, "What'd he look like?"

"He was about five-six with blue-jean shorts, a white T-shirt, beads in his hair, and he can run like a jackrabbit."

Here I am in Vegas. Don't know a soul. Got a Mountain Dew and a few pennies to my name. I can't even walk across the street and get the cheap motel room. I had nobody I could call and say, "Hey, can you send me fifty dollars?"

I was homeless. The first night I walked to a Walmart, dug some bubble wrap out of the trash, and slept on it. Didn't have a blanket or nothin'. Slept beneath a bush.

I still tried to get a job. Went to Labor Ready on Main Street. Hadn't shaved. Hadn't had a shower. I could smell myself. Plus my "dogs" were killing me. They were barking. I got problems with my feet from when I got hit with that RPG in Desert Storm.

Never got to the top of the Labor Ready list. Sat there every morning for three or four days and my name never got called.

Trying to get disability or VA benefits they run you through the wringer. At first I didn't want 'em. Didn't need 'em. Let that money go to somebody that needs it. I can walk, I can talk, I can work.

I've never had a problem getting a job, but in Vegas I couldn't get shit. It was a totally different world. Even McDonald's turned me down. Said I was overqualified.

I started stealing from Walmart and pawning the stuff. I knew that wasn't gonna last long. I was gonna go to jail and I didn't wanna do that, and it bothered me to steal, but I was trying to survive. Then I met this guy and he showed me panhandling. That was the hardest thing I've done in my life. Holding a sign and asking for help. I could always take care of myself, and for the first time I couldn't.

I said I'd never steal and I did. I said I'd never eat out of a trashcan. Well, I ate out of a trashcan too.

Jamie: I hated cops. They were the enemy, given my music-playing and drug-dealing ways. But when I got out of prison for selling weed, a friend of mine introduced me to this chick who worked for the Mississippi Bureau of Narcotics as a CI.

I said, "Dude, are you kidding me? Are you crazy?"

For some reason her and I hit it off and I ended up moving in with her. I don't know how it worked. She was everything I wasn't—a cowgirl, country-music loving, shit-kicking cop.

She was originally from Las Vegas and she moved back there around 1996. I flew out to visit her and see what Vegas was all about, and she talked me into moving there. I went back to Mississippi and packed everything I could into my car and drove out there in one day.

Me and my girlfriend were on meth. Our lives started to center around that. We had a nice house in Summerlin. We had cars, guitars, a pool table in the foyer, and she threw all of it away or sold it for drugs. Her boys were grown at that point and I knew they could take care of themselves. That was the deciding factor in me leaving her.

I went back to Mississippi and came back to Vegas a couple times. The last time I came back she met me at the airport, and I moved in with her and her boyfriend. Me and him were buddies. He was a cool guy. He only had one job all his life: scrapping. He could climb. He was like Spider-Man and we hit places all over Vegas, anything that got shut down during the recession. We met this African guy who had an illegal business that he ran out of his truck, and he'd come to wherever we were and weigh our stuff and buy it from us, then take it to California and sell it for four times what he paid for it.

We were making $400 or $500 a night. All we did was stay up smoking or shooting meth and scrapping, and the next day we gambled away the money we made.

The dead guy was in an apartment by the Hard Rock. Me and my ex's boyfriend were on one of our scrapping missions, and I pried the plywood from the window and slipped in— just a safety-check before I started breaking walls out. Had to make sure no one was there.

The first bedroom I walked into had a giant pile of old clothes in the middle of it. I kicked at it thinking there could be something under it. There was. I could see part of a human face, eyes wide open. I slowly uncovered a head.

The guy had been a gang member of some sort. He was covered in prison tats, looked like Aryan stuff. What was odd was that he was stacked up in pieces: torso, legs, arms, and the head on top. He didn't have any hands and they took out all his teeth to make it harder to ID him. There was no smell, which told me he hadn't been there long.

I sat down in front of this grisly scene and smoked a joint, then I got paranoid so I covered him back up and went out the same window, spray-painting everything I may have touched to eliminate my prints. I didn't want any part of whatever was going on there. I put some extra nails in the window boards and never set foot in that building again.

Phil: By the time I was in my mid-twenties, a few years after my dad was killed by the blinds guy, I decided to get my head out of my ass and get an automotive degree. I got all my certifications, which made me a master technician.

I worked as a mechanic in California for Kaiser Steel, then I went to another big company. I jumped around a lot because I was a commodity. I had skills and was getting paid union wages.

Eventually I took a job in Las Vegas with Fletcher Jones Toyota. I was their lead mechanic.

I was thinking, Hallelujah! That's the best way to explain how I felt about Vegas. With my mechanic's job and street smarts I knew I could thrive there. All those lights. All that money. All that opportunity.

I could've never guessed it would end up like it did.

THE STREETS

In the preceding chapters, the interviewees opened up about their earliest memory, childhood, and adulthood. Now, with some context, we can ask, "When and how did you become homeless?" Seemingly straightforward answers along the lines of "I got evicted," "I lost my job," and "I was addicted to crack" become more complex, as we know the circumstances surrounding that pivotal moment. We know, for example, why he or she became addicted to crack (or we can at least make a reasonable assumption).

This question about when and how they became homeless may not have elicited as many varied responses as the one about ending up in Vegas, but it did produce some surprises. See Knyck's sad story about Xanies, grannies, and guilt, and Ande's transition from McDonnell Douglas to McDonald's.

Sweeny: I was living in my car. Six-cylinder, 1994 Ford Mustang. Got to Vegas from Washington, didn't know anyone, and was trying to figure out what I was going to do. After a week or so my car broke down at the Excalibur. I'd leave it there during the day and at night I would sleep in it.

One night security knocked on the window and said, "You can't sleep here." I told them the car was broken down and they said, "Sorry. You have to go."

They kicked me off the property and told me not to come back. I grabbed what I could from the car and walked off and was officially on the street.

Shaggy: The first time I was homeless was in tenth grade. I wrote a paper about it in English class.

My mom and her boyfriend at the time were both in recovery. She was a constant relapser and it was proof to me that there was no chance of real recovery. She eventually moved out and I stayed and ended up getting a job and paying him rent. Since I was paying rent I thought I should have a say in what goes on in the house, and all I asked was that my mom didn't stay there.

I was lying on the couch eating Cheez-Its and drinking Dr. Pepper, and my mom knocked on the front door. She asked to speak to her ex-boyfriend and I said, "He doesn't wanna talk to you. You're not welcomed here."

She said, "If I'm not welcomed here how come I was here last night?"

I got upset about that and packed my bags and bounced.

There's an Alcoholics Anonymous club near Jones and Sahara, and at the time there was nothing behind it. After leaving my mom's ex-boyfriend's house, I slept in the desert there next to an old man named Paul. He had two mattresses stacked on each other and he gave me one of 'em.

The first night we broke into a doctor's office, found a bunch of alcohol, and drank it all. That night was a breeze; the morning was hard. I woke up in the heat, sick, no water, nowhere to go, and I remember thinking, What am I gonna do now?

Merch: I was living in Harbor Island apartments and I got 86'd for having too much traffic at my place. Three or four working girls stayed with me. I couldn't take them all with me on the streets, so I had to pick one and I picked wrong: Jessica.

The first night a customer of hers got us a room at the Wild Wild West. It was up to her to take care of the next night too. That morning she procrastinated and we had to check out because the payment was due at eleven and she didn't get back till one. I already had our stuff packed and out on the sidewalk.

I called a friend of a friend and he said he had a mobile home in the truck lot across the street. He said it was seventy-five dollars a week and didn't have power or water, but it did have a roof.

"I'll take it."

One of the girls that was staying with me at Harbor Island showed up on Tropicana and she moved in with us. They were working the truck lot, but that didn't last long. Security caught 'em and kicked us out, and that's when I became homeless.

Knyck: I was getting ready for my third semester at College of Southern Nevada and my aunt suggested—till this day my uncle says it was the worst thing she ever said to me—that I take a semester off. I don't know why she said that, but she thought it was a good idea. I took that semester off and lost my job at the Las Vegas Hilton. I was a lifeguard there, then became pool supervisor. One day at work I took three Xanie bars, and next thing I know my boss was standing over me with security guards.

I said, "What's going on?"

She said, "Can you come with me?" They showed me a video of me taking an ice cream cone from the employee dining room and painting my face with it. I had no recollection of doing that.

Feeling sorry for me, my grandmother gave me her Wells Fargo ATM card. She had $90,000 in the bank. "Knycky, I know you lost your job. If you need anything just take the money out. I trust you."

In two months I took out $10,000. I felt so shitty about that I chose to leave the family home and live on the streets. The funny thing was my grandmother didn't even know I'd taken the money.

Half Pint: When I was teaching in Texas I'd gone to rehab three or four times. I went to rehab in Vegas another thirteen. I kept going to rehab and moving schools, and my parents kept flying here from Nebraska and bailing me out. They came here in 2008 and said, "We're gonna try this one more time."

I went to Montevista Hospital and wasn't there forty-eight hours before I bolted. They give you a cab wherever you're going when you leave, so I came back to my apartment and everything was gone. My parents had packed it and put it in storage and left town. I went to the apartment office and they said, "You're no longer welcomed here. It's been suggested to us that if you reappear we have you 86'd from the property and call the cops."

I had my ID, twenty dollars in my purse, the clothes on my back, and my little rolling suitcase, and I started walking down Charleston. I stopped at Walgreens to get a refill of a script—100 Lortabs—and paid for it with the twenty. I took a bunch of the pills and somehow managed to make it further down Charleston. I got somebody to let me use their phone and I called Mom and Dad.

"This is your daughter. Where are you? I left Monte ..."

I didn't get the whole word out before they hung up on me. I called back and my dad said, "Unless you're in Montevista we have nothing to say to you! We're done!"

"Where's my shit? What'd you do with it?"

"It's in storage. You won't see any of it till you get your life together."

Pretty Boy Steve: I was still in the hotel industry. I was working for Bob Stupak and living with Mom and Dad, and they were really tired of me and I don't blame 'em. I went for the quick cash. Some girl approached me, led me on, and next thing I know I'm cashing two payroll checks for $1,000 each at a casino. Six months later I got stopped by the police and charged with felony counts of forgery, burglary, and robbery. It was my first time really being in trouble.

Six months after that I got caught with drugs and got another felony conviction. It just proceeded to get worse after that.

All this was hard on my parents and friends, and one day I said the hell with this. I'm not gonna ask to stay with anyone else or for anything more. I started sleeping in this alley near where I grew up, by the Marie Callender's at Sahara and Sixth. Freezing to death with one blanket over my body.

David: I was in the Air Force for ten years, three of them in England. I wanted to stay in twenty, but my wife and I fought like cats and dogs. Finally I put in a special request to get away from her and I got assigned to Korea. My wife and kids were in base housing in Louisiana till I completed my assignment, but she was messing around with some dude. We both messed around, but I was ready to kill her when I found out she'd messed around on me.

My wife had made enemies on base. She was combative. I got called back from Korea to address the problems at my house. They put me on emergency leave. I'd already been demoted because of the problems with me and my wife and for being late for work, and eventually I got kicked out.

I sent the family back to Shreveport and stayed in Korea for another couple months, then went to Sacramento and ran into a guy I was stationed with in Korea. He'd gotten kicked out too. We ended up on the streets and the first thing he did was show me how to smoke crack.

That was the beginning of the end.

Phil: My wife was insecure with me being at Fletcher Jones, working on strippers' cars and stuff like that. She bones out and I'm like, Fuck it! I was hanging with a buddy and we were drinking and he hands me the pipe, and I went on a binge for a month. Didn't show up for work, didn't pay rent, got evicted. Didn't do nothin' but smoke crack.

I ended up by the old Showboat casino on Boulder Highway. I was sleeping in a park over there, trying to avoid the cops. This was 2001. The worst year of my life. My 9/11.

Misty: I gave birth to a daughter shortly after I moved to Vegas to be with her father. Ended up confronting him and his mother about his drug use. She kicked me out and wouldn't let me take my kid. Claimed I was a drug-addicted, piece-of-crap mom who couldn't hold a job. I had two jobs at the time—Albertsons and a dry cleaner—and I came home every night and took care of my kid.

I ended up on the streets and running into a few people who showed me the ropes: how to fly a sign and where to sleep; be careful who you trust; don't show any weakness.

The first time I was homeless I was thirteen years old. I've been on and off the streets most of my life, but this was different. It's a different speed in Vegas. Faster, more in-depth than what I was used to in Oregon. This was the big time.

Stephen: I was barely twenty-one when I got a job as a waiter at the Aladdin. This was before Wayne Newton bought it. Old gangsters owned it. We had three great restaurants: a steakhouse, an Italian joint, and a fish house. I wouldn't even give people menus. I'd just say, "What do you wanna eat?"

Twelve years later I was a captain and maître d', and I'd wear a tuxedo and shiny, patent-leather shoes, but I couldn't drive to work without a beer between my legs and a joint between my fingers.

One day I woke up and I wasn't putting on my tuxedo and shiny shoes and going to the Aladdin. I was working at the carwash across from UNLV. Even that job interfered with my drinking, so I lost it too.

The university had this big grassy area. Soccer fields, I guess. I just curled up there next to the fence. The sprinklers came on around five in the morning and woke me up and got me wet. That was my first night of having nowhere to go.

I got to know some of the working girls on the streets. They'd say, "Steve, make sure the john sees you see me getting into the car." That way he knows someone has seen 'em together and he won't hurt 'em. I wasn't a pimp, but when the girls were done they'd come back to my motel room, when I could afford one, and we'd get crack and smoke. I didn't bother them or anything.

I did get close to one girl. I liked her a lot. She was married to an abusive husband. I got to know her because I had drugs, enough to sell to get a weekly, and we stayed in them together. Then all of a sudden she was gone.

A year and a half later I'm on the corner of Oakey and Las Vegas Boulevard waiting to score and I hear someone yell my name. It was her.

I said, "What happened? Where've you been?"

She said a couple nights after she left the weekly she got into this car. These guys took her to a hotel on Paradise. She didn't know what happened, but three days later she woke up half dead with a broomstick up her ass.

Then she said, "There's my ride. I gotta go."

And she hopped into a car.

Easy E: I stayed in that apartment on Sierra Vista—the one where I met the hot blonde—for two months, and worked a free month's rent out of them by telling them my mom was sending money, but then they kicked me out. I didn't know what to do. I stashed my stuff behind an abandoned building on Sierra Vista near Maryland Parkway and I was sleeping behind the building at night. This guy looks down from the roof and says, "Dude, I wouldn't stay down there. Gangbangers sell crack across the way and a lot of people smoke it here. Come up on the roof with me." He lowered a ladder and I climbed up.

The next day we walked through the Boulevard Mall and Jason—that was his name—scooped change out of the fountains, then went across the street to a bank and got wrappers to put the coins in and we cashed them at 7-Eleven. We got hot dogs, soda, nachos, whatever we wanted. Then we went to CVS to steal cigarettes. He taught me the ropes, especially how to boost, and I became proficient at it.

Me and Jason decided we wanted to go to the Strip because I knew how to hustle credits. I said, "We gotta get dressed up," so we went to Copeland Sports. I'm proficient in criminal law because, well, I'm a criminal, and I knew a petty larceny was $249.99 or under and grand larceny was $250 or more. As we were stealing clothes I was adding it up. When we got to exactly $249.99 we started to walk out, but a guard grabbed me and slammed me against the wall and handcuffed me.

I said, "Dude, you got me fair and square! You don't have to rough me up!"

Jason was in the golf department taking on the other guard. They were swinging and throwing clubs at each other.

They finally got us both handcuffed in the office and the cops came. Jason was wanted for grand theft auto and he gave them his cousin's name. They were the same height and build, but his cousin had blue eyes and Jason's were brown. The total merchandise we'd stolen was under $250, but one of the cops noticed a backpack we'd brought in, which showed intent to steal and made it a felony. Then they started telling Jason his eyes weren't blue.

They took us to jail, got our fingerprints, and we went to court that Tuesday and got released before the prints were processed. We ran from the charges. I'm a jackrabbit. I don't stay around for nothing.

Iron: The second Christmas I was in Vegas it was cold and rainy. I was on the Strip pushing cars out of the water to get spare change, and I ran into my sister and her husband by chance. They were visiting from Oklahoma. I was doing bad. I'd just lost a job driving pedicabs because they outlawed them, and I lost the place where I was staying too. I was living behind a dumpster on the Strip. I told my sister I wanted to come home and she said, "Our car's full." We haven't spoken since.

Jodie, 54, lived in the drains for seven years with her boyfriend Eddie. Raised in California, she dropped out of school in the tenth grade and got married and had a kid before turning eighteen. During a recession in the early eighties, she and her husband and kids moved from California to Utah and eventually ended up in Vegas: Me and my husband were living with my adult daughter. We had a little apartment. I couldn't stand living with her. She was and still is a bitch. Too much tension, too much fighting with me and my husband and her.

He beat the crap outta me one night and kicked me out. I had a small bag of clothes and found a place to sleep behind a warehouse, a dumpster area with no dumpster in it. That was in North Las Vegas. I went to bum some change for beer and ran into Eddie.

We had a few beers and were talking. He had a camp just down from mine. I didn't even know he was there. He had blankets and stuff so I said, "Can I stay with you?"

We've been together ever since.

Eddie, 55, grew up in rural New York. He dropped out of school in the ninth grade and his parents kicked him out of the house when he was seventeen. He moved to Las Vegas circa 1980, because he had family in the city, and he worked warehouse jobs intermittently: I was homeless, but in denial. I had a job and was living paycheck to paycheck, buying cigarettes and beer. That's all I could afford. And ramen. I'd buy a case of it and that was my food for the week.

I'd go into 7-Eleven and get a can of beer to help me sleep. I was standing in line and Jodie comes bopping up. "Gimme some money!"

I said, "Tell you what. I'll get a twelve-pack and me and you can share it. I'll meet you on the side of the building."

She was a loon, but after a few beers that looniness was pretty interesting. Everything about her is out there. It was fun. I was alone anyway so I thought, Why not camp together?

Cyndi: My daughters' dad wouldn't get a job. He'd just sit on the couch and drink beer. I was on welfare and food stamps and taking care of the kids. I didn't have much money, so I started dealing meth out of the house and dipping into the extras. Eventually it caught up with me and I lost my kids to CPS.

When I lost my kids, I lost my welfare check and I was put on the streets. I drank. I OD'd on meth. I was down to seventy pounds. I was trying to punish myself for what happened to my little brother, father, and kids. I felt like I'd murdered seven people.

At one point I was living in a cardboard box in some bushes in Davis, California. Every so often the cops would see me walking down the street and arrest me on false charges, just so I could go to jail and get some food.

I was walking across the street to get some liquor and a car came flying off the freeway and hit me. I was in a coma for four days. My brain was bleeding. My leg was shattered and my body was hamburger meat. They thought I was going to be a vegetable.

After I got out of the hospital I started going to AA and I tried really hard to stay sober. That's where I met Rick. He kept staring at me at a meeting. I was like, What's this dude's problem? He had a girl sitting next to him and I assumed it was his girlfriend, so I thought he was rude. A couple weeks later she comes up and says, "He's just a friend and he likes you," and I started having a different view of him. I made him my coffee server at a meeting I was chairing and it went from there.

Melinda: The first time I became homeless I was pregnant with my son Alex. My children's father had a Cadillac and he had me thinking we were going to a weekly or a hotel, but he just parked the car.

I said, "Why aren't we going into our place?"

"Because we're homeless."

We had our dog and our other son and all our stuff with us, and I just sat there and cried.

We stayed in day shelters and churches for a few years, and I got pregnant with my daughter Christianni. I'm not proud of it, but I got knocked up in a church. That's why I named her that.

Ande: Y2K came along and the world was going crazy. I had money in my 401(k), so I decided to take time off from working and spend it with my dog and just read and relax. My dad and brother, who were living in Las Vegas, said, "Why don't you come out here?"

I hadn't seen much of my family in the last several years, and I thought it'd be a good time to reconcile with them and try something new.

I sized up Vegas real quick. Eighteen- to twenty-one-year-olds with little or no education were making $75,000 a year, and they wanted to pay me ten bucks an hour to work tech support for UPS.

The last job I had here was at McDonald's. I went from Mickey D's, which is what we called McDonnell Douglas, to Mickey D's. I was a cashier and stockroom worker at a McDonald's on the Strip. It was the hardest job I ever had; it was the busiest McDonald's in the city. But then the recession hit and I got laid off. Vegas went from 5 percent unemployment to 16 percent.

I got kicked outta my apartment and started paying people fifty dollars a week to stay on their porches. Then, for whatever reason, they'd kick me out.

Finally a friend said, "Why don't you go down to the tunnel?"

DISCOVERING THE DRAINS PART II

Melinda: The father of my children promised he would pay for a hotel room for the week, but he disappeared, and I ended up homeless on Fremont Street. Girls I'd meet on the street would take me in, weekly motel to weekly motel. Sometimes I'd sleep behind the post office. I slept in the park across from the courthouse under a bench. I had nowhere to go and was by myself. I'd lost my kids to CPS and didn't want to be around my children's father.

I met Manny on Fremont. I was at the old Atomic Liquors with my friend Rachel. I hung around with a bunch of Native Americans and he was one of their friends and he was like, "Who's that?"

I wasn't looking for a relationship, but his eye—he's blind in his left one from getting hit with a beer bottle—caught my attention and he was warm and I felt safe. I didn't know he was homeless because he took me to this apartment. Well, it was a motel room, but when you're homeless that's an apartment to you. Then one day he couldn't pay for it and said, "I stay at this other place too, and you can meet my friends."

I'm thinking, Right on. I got a guy that has his own place. Maybe he can help me get back on my feet. But he took me to this ditch and I started freaking out because I have a history of being raped.

"You're going to kill me, aren't you?"

He said, "No. I forgot my rope and shovel." He was drunk and laughing.

"It's not funny, dude."

"Let me get out my key," and he pulled out a flashlight. "I know this looks weird, but you'll meet some good people and it's safe and better than being on the street."

It was really dark. From staying with my mom when I was young, I don't like the dark. It smelled like sewage and we walked around these black puddles. Finally I saw a light and I heard people laughing. They had headlamps on, decorations on the walls, beds, and I'm like, What the heck is this? Manny walked me to the back, where his camp was, and I met everybody and they were friendly.

"Don't be scared," he said. "Everything will be okay."

Maddie: The first time I went down there I was scared shitless. I was fourteen years old. I was like, What the hell? My girlfriend Olivia was more ballsy than I was. She was the one that pushed me to go down there to hang out. I'd already drunk aboveground with the people who lived down there, and I was comfortable with them, but I was scared someone would jump out of the dark and whack us with a baseball bat or something.

We went in the back way and walked forever. I'm like, Oh my God! What have I gotten myself into? It was super dark and there was only one flashlight between six of us. There was a bonfire going. I could smell it.

We finally got to the camp, and Captain Jack was sitting in front of the fire, and we all sat down with him. Gretchen and Dakota, this traveling couple with dreadlocks, were playing the banjo and singing, and everybody was drinking and having a good time. There were really positive vibes.

Szmauz: I have no idea who decked me when I was giving that guy hot dogs or what his issue was, but apparently that wasn't the first time that had happened around there. There were people in that neighborhood who'd harass the homeless.

But the next day, as I was rummaging through dumpsters on meth, I was like, I should check out that tunnel. I took my flashlight there and started exploring, and I realized no one ever went down there. I was staying up for several days at a time and I'd just crash anywhere, and I was paranoid the cops were out to get me.

The tunnels seemed promising. No cop was gonna go down there.

Ricky Lee: They started tearing down the abandoned hotel where I was staying and paying rent, so I took my stuff and went to the tunnels.

The tunnels weren't new at that time. They'd been there for a few years, but nobody had been in them. I said, Why not? They're covered. You're out of the sun. You're outta sight. Me and these two other guys, Red and Ervin, were the first to move in.

The tunnel is six feet high and ten feet wide and cobwebs covered it wall to wall. We had to take a stick and cut the webbing to get through. We'd only make it 100 feet and we'd get scared and tired.

Then one day Ervin and his dog went all the way through. He threw golf balls into the darkness and the dog chased 'em and broke the webs.

Tommy: After ditching weed in that high-speed chase in California, I got busted with some in Vegas. A quarter pound. I went to jail for only sixty days because the judge dropped it down to a misdemeanor, but during that time I lost everything—my apartment, truck, tools. When I was released I didn't have shit except for the clothes I was wearing, and I ended up on the corner of Trop and Valley View. I asked a guy for spare change so I could get some beer. I guess I looked a little rough because he handed me his wallet and said, "Please don't hurt me!"

"I just want some change, man. I don't want your wallet."

He handed me a few bucks and I went into the store and bought a six-pack.

I was up on the railroad tracks drinking by myself and I ran into somebody and gave him one of the beers. He said, "I live in the tunnels," so that's where I ended up going.

His name was Face and he had a girlfriend named Colleen. He showed me his little spot, broke out some crack, and I smoked with them. That's how I ended up down there.

Iron: Not long after I ran into my sister and her husband on the Strip, I migrated over by the Wild Wild West. I made me a little hooch aboveground next to the truck stop. I was there for a few months and kept getting harassed by the police. The other homeless folks in the area said, "Why don't you come to the tunnels?"

I said, "Ain't no way I'm going to the tunnels!"

I'd heard about them and what went on in 'em: somebody owed somebody some money and went down there and beat the dude up and burned out his camp; it's so dark you can't see nothin', and I don't like the dark no way. I didn't wanna be involved in all that crap. Didn't want no part of it.

But finally they talked me into it and I went into the one behind the Budget Suites.

Becky: Me and Zero knew some people who had an apartment and we stayed with them awhile, but they were behind on their rent and ended up losing the apartment. We stayed at Harbor Island for a bit. Too much money was going to drugs and gambling and we lost that place. We were huffing around town with all our bags, and that's when Zero took me to the tunnels.

I'm thinking, I've been in crappy places before. I can handle this. I don't know; I just did whatever Zero told me to. I wasn't about to leave him there and go back to Utah. We were gonna stick together.

Eddie: Me and Jodie were downtown trying to figure things out. I got a job building trusses and we had a little hooch on the side of the railroad tracks. We lived in that till the railroad cops came and kicked it down, threw away our IDs, and took us to jail. I lost my job because of that.

When we got out we went back to the hooch and grabbed what we could and I said, "Screw this! There's nothing for us downtown. We have to get away from here." Every time we turned around we were getting thrown to the ground by the cops.

We packed our backpacks and started down the tracks. As we were walking the sole of my sneaker ripped off.

Jodie said, "We have to turn around."

"I ain't turning around!"

Twenty feet further there was a shoebox on the tracks, and I opened it and there was a brand-new pair of sneakers in it. I tried them on and they fit perfectly, so we kept trekking.

We got to Russell Road and went down alongside the tracks and found a tunnel. We stayed in the opening for a few months, then it started to get cold and we had to go in deeper. We found a nook that dead-ended. It was filled with branches and garbage, and we cleaned it out and moved in.

Jamie: My ex kicked me and her boyfriend out and we ended up in the Klondike Hotel just before they knocked it down. The place was fenced off and we destroyed it. Knocked the walls out and scrapped everything that was worth anything. Kregg came up and introduced himself to me. Asked if he could have one of the mattresses.

"Where you taking it to?"

He led me past the "Welcome to Fabulous Las Vegas" sign carrying a box spring on his back. Right across the boulevard and into the tunnel. I was like, Wow! This is cool!

They had camps in there, but hardly anyone had a mattress. We started moving whole rooms from the Klondike down there. Everybody had carpet and beds and armoires. That's when I started to get to know Kregg and Skip and where I met Ricky Lee and Zero.

Zero walked up to me. Didn't even know my name. He'd just hit a lick in one of the casinos, and I was with Kregg and he gives him twenty bucks. He said to me, "I don't know you, man, but I'm Zero. I'm from N'Orleans." And he handed me twenty dollars too.

I was like, "Thanks. I'm Jamie. I'm from Mississippi."

"No shit?"

It was an instant friendship.

Pretty Boy Steve: When I worked for Stupak I met this guy Gary who used to come into the hotel. Just some random, homeless, drug-addict dude. We started talking and I asked him where he stayed and he said the tunnels. I was close to being homeless, so he took me down and showed me where he lived, but I didn't move in with him because it was scary. The first question you have is, "What do you do when it rains?"

But it seemed like a good place to be by yourself and do drugs or whatever you gotta do and chill out for a while, and

PRETTY BOY STEVE

before I knew it I had a bed down there. And then a chair. And then a table. All of a sudden you're comfortable.

Gary didn't want anybody else there, but he didn't have a choice because he wasn't a badass. I went down and ten or eleven other people followed.

Kat, 54, lived in the drains off and on for ten years with her boyfriend Pretty Boy Steve. She grew up in Florida and, after graduating from a private school, got married and began waitressing and bartending. Many years later, she moved to Las Vegas to attend Le Cordon Bleu culinary school: The economy went bad and I lost my funding at

Cordon Bleu four classes short of graduating. I didn't know what to do. I couldn't afford my apartment so I moved in with some other students. There was a whole bunch of us in one place. It was horrible. I looked forward to the weekends, when I could get away from there. Basically I was couch-surfing.

One weekend I was at a bus stop in Henderson, trying to get away from my roommates. This guy started talking to me and asked if I wanted to make some money.

"Sorry," I said, "I don't do that."

"In the casinos," he said.

He started telling me about credit hustling and how we can make all this money, but first we have to get his friend Steve. We got on the bus and got off by the Rio, and he took me into the tunnels.

I was like, What the heck is going on? He turned his flashlight off. He thought it was funny. I said, "That's not funny. I don't appreciate it."

He lived pretty far back. We kept walking, and when we got there Steve was asleep. His friend woke him up and introduced me to him. I just sat there. I was quiet. I was so scared.

At first I thought Steve was a jerk. We had to wait for his jeans to dry, and all I wanted to do was run outta that tunnel. His jeans were hanging in a manhole, which had a tiny bit of sunshine coming through. It took forever.

We finally left and went to the Stratosphere, and I started seeing what credit hustling was all about.

We got to the Wynn and Steve's friend was showing us a $280 ticket he had taken from somebody. The man came up behind him screaming for security and wouldn't let the friend go. Steve looked at me and said, "It's time for us to leave."

We went outside and waited for his friend, but he never came out, so we kept walking. He took me to the Bellagio and I couldn't believe it. It was so beautiful—the flowers, the artwork on the ceiling, the dancing fountains out front.

Rick, 43, lived in the tunnels with his wife Cyndi. He grew up in California and Nevada in the biker scene and never finished high school. As a young adult, he periodically worked part-time jobs and used and sold drugs: My mom called me from Las Vegas and said she had emphysema. "I'm not doing well," she said. "I'm having suicidal thoughts. I need your help." So in 2006 Cyndi and I came out to Vegas to help her.

I became my mother's in-home healthcare provider. Taking her to doctor's appointments, getting her medications, taking her blood pressure several times a day. I also got to have a relationship with her I never had before. I got to know her.

In 2010, when my mom passed away, we took all our stuff to my friend's place and moved in with him. He was like a brother to me. A stand-up guy. The first night Cyndi and I went out to party we came back to an empty apartment. He rented a moving truck and stole everything we owned. He also called the cops and said the place was in his name and that we had to go.

We had one bicycle and two backpacks between us and were put out on the street.

The police were cracking down on the homeless in the area, and we walked around for a few days, trying to find a place to lay down. I literally stopped to tie my shoe and a cop yelled over his PA system, "Keep moving or you're going to jail!"

Cyndi said we need to get out of sight and get some rest and come up with a plan. She said let's go to that tunnel you were telling me about where your friend TK is staying. We can sit down for a minute and get some sleep.

Sweeny: After getting kicked off the Excalibur's property, I was looking for different places to crash when I was wandering around the city recycling. Eventually I found a spot under the train tracks by the Rio. I could hide my stuff and sleep there and not many people were around.

One day I saw some people, nicely dressed, walking outta the nearby tunnels. It was Steve and Kat. They came up by the tracks and I started talking to 'em. That was my first contact with the group that was already in there.

That summer I moved into the tunnels to get out of the heat. I ended up crashing at the front, so the group that was deeper in there would walk by and they got to know me. I did that for a couple months before Steve and Kat said I could move farther in, back where they all were.

LIFE BELOW

When I read about the fugitive Timmy "T.J." Weber using underground flood channels to evade police, I decided to follow his trail, never considering that the drains might be inhabited. I couldn't make that connection; it was too remote an idea for a young man from the middle-class South. I expected to find debris, graffiti scrawls, and maybe a feral animal or two, but not people. People don't live in dark, dank concrete boxes that can fill at one foot per minute with floodwater.

Exploring the drains with my *CityLife* colleague Josh Ellis, I discovered that people do live belowground. Hundreds of them, perhaps thousands. (A specific number is impossible to pinpoint, as there are 300 miles of tunnels and the population is in constant flux.) As Josh and I interviewed the inhabitants, the idea of camping in the drains began to make sense. They are ready-made, reliable shanties—a floor, two walls, and a ceiling. They provide shelter from the extreme Mojave heat and cold. Some of them are dry for weeks, even months. In a tourist town that has criminalized homelessness, the tunnel residents remain largely out of sight and out of mind.

Life in the drains contains common themes—trauma, addiction, resourcefulness—but the day-to-day experience can vary wildly. Some residents, including Pretty Boy Steve and Kat, prefer sprawling, sectioned campsites. Others, like Tommy, keep it simple. Some have part-time or full-time jobs. Others have hustles. Some drink. Others smoke crack.

Questions, no doubt, remain: Do the tunnel residents bathe? If so, where and how? Where do they use the restroom? Are there rules in the drains? If so, who enforces them? How much money can a hustler make? What is life like for women, who make up roughly 25 percent of the population?

This chapter aims to answer these and other related questions.

Vegas Dee: Me and Ned were at the Diamond Inn, the motel on the Strip with the pink elephant in front of it. We were in a nice back room and I had money and dope in my bra. We started running low and we had an argument and I said, "I'm not staying here anymore. I'm going to where I know my dope is and I know the people won't judge me."

The first night in the tunnel was very intriguing. I thought something might pop off, but it was just people constantly coming and going. We took it all in and finally fell asleep. When we woke up they were like, "Hey, you need anything?"

We didn't have to call anybody or go anywhere to get drugs.

We pushed our way in and ended up taking one side of the tunnel. Just macking it out and making it home. I remember one time the police came down and this cop was sitting in a recliner chair and I said, "Would you like some lemonade, officer?"

He said, "Vegas Dee, this is bullshit. Your place is nicer than mine."

Pops, Jake, Tony, Ned. We'd sit there for hours and share stories of our friends and families. We bonded. We laughed.

We felt free. We took care of each other. I'd go and turn tricks and get food. Everybody did something for each other.

A lot of times I didn't even turn tricks. I'd just take the money and leave because I would never see that person again. I burnt the ones who were crazy and tried to lock me in the room or hurt me.

That's part of the reason I went to the tunnels—to get away from those people. To hide. Nobody would come down there looking for me. They'd be like, Wow! She just walked into a freakin' tunnel!

I'd say, "I just burned somebody!" And all the guys would go outside and say, "What's up, dude?"

"Um, I'm looking for a girl."

"There's no girl down here."

What are they gonna do? Come down there and look for me?

Phil: What the hell? What did I do to deserve this? What am I gonna do now? Those were my first thoughts when I ended up down there. I just sat in the dark thinking, What the fuck? I'd just lost my last $600 playing blackjack, so I was pretty pissed.

But my dad was a strong man, and he told me no matter how many times life knocks you down you have to get up. I had that in mind. I knew I'd be all right.

Living under the streets of Vegas and having to come up to do what you gotta do is tough, because you have to live with what you've done down there and be able to function up above and look right. You can't look like a bum crawling out of a hole. You won't survive. Who's gonna do anything for you? You have to go up there with a tin cup and pity yourself, and the people throw pennies at you.

Ande: The tunnel was across from a few apartment complexes. One of them was drug-head city. It was an old 1950s resort for actors and actresses who wanted to visit Vegas and not stay in a casino.

The maintenance crew used to clean out the apartments, and if they found extra furniture it would end up in the tunnel. They, at times, would live or hang out down there. Everybody around there knew about the tunnel. It was a well-established place to sleep and do drugs.

After moving from porch to porch for several years, it was just a slight graduation down for me. It was peaceful. Nobody bugged me. I could get my beer at any street-corner store and go down there and listen to music, meditate, and talk to God.

I wasn't down there long before somebody told me there was hot water coming out of a nearby fire hydrant. I could bath and wash my hair every day, so I was always clean. That was important to me. I could also walk to any store I needed to, whether it was Circle K, the liquor store, or 7-Eleven—whoever had the cheapest beer. I could go to the library and take care of business: call 1-800 numbers, make sure my food stamps were set up, stuff like that.

I've always looked like a guy. People would come down and attack me and steal from me, thinking I was a man, and I'd simply say, "You're gonna take it out on a woman, huh?" That was my defense.

They'd say, "Oh my God! I'm sorry! I had no idea."

I never flew a sign. I didn't like doing that. I'd simply go up to people at a gas station or the parking lot of Smith's and say, "Can you please spare twenty-five cents for the bus?" Whether they said yes or no I'd say, "Thank you very much.

Have a great day." Over a five-year span I made almost $20,000.

My limit was ten dollars a day. I stopped at ten because that's all I needed for a pack of cigarettes and a couple beers.

The transistor radio kept me alive. You had nothing to do but twiddle your thumbs. I was so serious about these two NPR shows that everyone knew not to bother me on Saturday night. *Prairie Home Companion* with Garrison Keillor—if I can get his entire set someday as a Christmas present that would be the best thing ever. And *Wait Wait . . . Don't Tell Me!*, especially when Rosie O'Donnell was on.

Both shows were on around six o'clock. I'd get a beer and go back to the tunnel and I'd tell anyone who came to visit, "Dude, you have to come back some other time."

One Shoe Sue: It was a tunnel near Valley View and Trop. I just remember going back into it and my head was really loud. I couldn't keep it quiet. The mattress that was in there smelled like piss, and it was really cold down there. I remember going to the Rebel store and begging for gloves. A taxi driver took pity on me and bought me a pair of gardening gloves.

I was either getting high, eating at Wendy's, taking a shower at the truck stop, or turning tricks. If I was tricking I was on Ali Baba Lane by the old Americana Inn. That was my track because there was a lot of trucks back there at three or four in the morning. I'd walk that area from three to six.

Shaggy: It was like a weight had been lifted off my shoulders. The tunnel was away from the world, and these guys were cool and they explained the rules to me and who was welcomed and who was not. They made me feel at home.

One rule is you don't touch anyone else's camp. You get caught in someone's spot and it's bad news. There was also a call to come in the tunnel. Ours was the old punk-rock word "oi." If you didn't say it and get the call back you were entering at your own risk.

There were fifteen to twenty of us at any given time. There was a sixteen-year-old runaway, Maddie, all the way up to Baldy, who was forty-seven. Jabber Jaw had been there fifteen years. He's a good guy, but he's everything about the tunnels incarnate. Friendly but unforgiving. Nice but ruthless.

My hustle at first was panhandling. I started out making a hundred dollars a day, but there were days I made $400 or $500. I think it was because of the improvisation I'd learned in high school. Depending on who I was talking to I'd have different stories as to why I was there. It also had to do with longevity. I was known in the area.

Later I sold drugs out of the tunnels. There are little drainage ditches and metal grates in parking lots. I'd ride the tunnels on a bike with a light and an Obama phone, and I'd sell drugs through the grates. I'd tell the buyer to act like they were tying their shoe and to pass the money and take the product. I never made money doing it, but I got my drugs for free.

Jodie: I wasn't freaked out because I was with Eddie. I felt safe. It was nice actually. Before we lived in cardboard boxes, so this nook was like a freakin' condo.

Nobody else would go in that tunnel. They called it the "Devil's Tunnel" because so many people had been killed there. They'd drive off the curve on Industrial Road and land right outside the tunnel. Other homeless people would tease us. "Y'all seen any ghosts? Heard any strange noises?"

Eddie: Right before we moved in, there was a man up on the street putting a stuffed animal and flowers on the guardrail post. His daughter had just died there.

Me and Jodie lived in that nook for five years before we realized no water went up into it. One day it was snowing and raining. We were stuck, but the water never touched our camp.

We were so cold we took our shoes off to try to walk out. The water was two feet deep. I went in first and said, "Holy shit! You gotta be kidding me!" It was ice cold. I turned around quick and we just sat there and watched everything float by.

Half Pint: I was scared shitless. I got fucked up and was raped numerous times by a group of men. When I came to, I started trying to be Miss Martial Artist and I was raped again. I passed out. When I woke up they weren't there and I went through their stuff and stole their pills and pipes. Big mistake. I went deeper into the tunnel, but they found me and beat me up.

They said, "That'll teach you not to do that again!" Then they pulled three of my fingernails off with a roach clip. I didn't learn from that either. I kept stealing from 'em. That cost me two teeth.

Pretty Boy Steve: I was hooked on heroin. Kat was drinking for good reasons. She was recently divorced, had lost her son, and had dropped out of culinary school, and now she was homeless and living in a tunnel. I didn't hold the drinking against her and she didn't hold what I was doing against me, and we fell in love.

She took a shine to the camp. It's something we both enjoyed doing together—going out and finding stuff and bringing it back to our home.

KAT AND PRETTY BOY STEVE

When I lay my head down at night I like to be comfortable; that requires a nice bed. That was our first priority, and they're easy to find in Vegas. The area where we lived had a lot of warehouses, and if there's a small stain or tear in a mattress into the trash it goes. We had our pick. The first one we had was a $5,000 king-sized mattress. It took five of us to get it down there and put it where we wanted it.

Two days later the county came and threw it away with the rest of our stuff.

When I get up in the morning I like to relax, put myself together, take a look in the mirror, and say, "What are you gonna do today? Make a cup of coffee? Read? Work?"

Kat and I were credit hustlers, so being clean was imperative. We got a big tub and washed clothes in it and sat in it and washed up. We had a water jug that we used as a shower. A mirror that went floor to ceiling. We took our job seriously and did quite well at it.

Kat: It became a challenge to see what we could find to make our camp better, to make it more comfortable, and we always found all kinda things. We were like, "That would be good in the living-room area." You'd find a piece of wood with a cool pattern on it in a dumpster, and you'd wonder if it would look nice over the bed. It was like interior design on a really tight budget.

It was tough being a couple down there because everybody was looking to upgrade. They wanted to upgrade their camp or their boyfriend or girlfriend or whatever. Everybody wanted what you had. It was terrible; you couldn't make friends. You didn't know who you could trust, but that was good for me and Steve in some ways, because it brought us closer together.

Rick: I became an efficient dumpster diver. We were right behind Burlington and they occasionally threw out pallets. The water would come through the tunnel without warning and we would use the pallets to walk on. We'd hit all the apartment complexes in the surrounding neighborhoods, pulling anything out of the dumpsters we could use. We learned what stores threw away food, and we'd find milk crates and put our bed on top of them to get away from the water, scorpions, and spiders.

If we needed something I'd pray to find it and usually I would. All of this to help avoid the reality that we were homeless, that we were living in a tunnel. Whatever we could find to make it seem more like home, the less real it made the experience.

When me and Cyndi first went into the tunnel there was TK and his girlfriend Melissa. A few other people would stay there from time to time. This big Indian who went by the name RIP. This little transsexual kid Pixie. They'd been frequenting that tunnel off and on for a few years before we came around.

The history of that tunnel, TK had told me, was sometimes it would be just him and other times a bunch of people would show up. I knew from day one that's what these tunnels were for: a refuge for homeless people. I saw tons of people around me who seemed to have less than we had, and we always tried to welcome them in.

I put on sweats to get ready to go to sleep and sat up on our bed Indian style and this scorpion walked across my pant leg. I guess it had been in my sweats when I put them on. It was a mom and she was transporting these tiny, transparent babies on her back. Fourteen or fifteen of 'em.

Cyndi got stung three times. I got stung twice, though I didn't tell her about it. I didn't want her to worry.

Tommy: My camp was simple. I didn't have a lot of possessions. The first time I did, it flooded and I lost 'em all, so I gave up on that. I had a backpack and whatever could fit into it: clean clothes, socks, and a nice pair of shoes, so I could go into the casinos and party.

I'd go to a casino and leave the backpack with a bellman. They'd keep it for a few days, then I'd come back, pick it up, and give them a dollar or two and go to another casino and leave it there. It was safer there than in the tunnel.

Maddie: I was the only girl for the longest time. At one point there was another girl, a pregnant woman. She was from Boston and had a strong accent. The baby daddy wasn't around from the start and she was close to eight months pregnant when we met her. She seemed to be running away from something—her baby daddy, her family, or both. She had a boyfriend that was also homeless and he was in jail, so she came and stayed with us until he got out. She did heroin and meth while pregnant and would sleep with anyone for dope.

She left before she gave birth—disappeared without saying goodbye—but I didn't mind being the only girl down there. I've always gotten along better with guys. In some ways, Knyck and Shaggy and Old Man Rob were like my brothers. None of 'em ever tried to force themselves on me. They protected me. They were the best group of guys I could've asked for.

Knyck: When I met Maddie down there she was fifteen. I was like, Why the hell is this girl here? She didn't seem to belong.

I felt sorry for her. I tried to get her food. It was inspiring because the guys didn't try to do anything to her. That's how I knew it was a good place. That tunnel and the group of people in it were special.

Easy E: There was an average of ten to fifteen people in our tunnel. We had a guy named Sharky, a piece of shit, big-time robber, in-and-out-of-jail type guy. We had Chris, a Puerto Rican who worked construction and was absolutely terrified that everybody was a cop when he was high. He looked like he was on steroids. Roid rage mixed with meth paranoia. Brian, a straight-up bully. "Give me some money or dope or I'm gonna beat the shit outta you!" Manny. Melinda. Phil.

Pretty Boy Steve. Kat. Sweeny. At any given time we could have twenty to twenty-five people there.

The rules were simple. Don't take without asking. Don't come down and flaunt what you got. If you got a bag of dope and you're flaunting it you better share it. If you don't you'll get a lot of resentment and people will say you're not getting shit from them the next time they score. Or worse.

But I can only think of one real hard, solid ass-whooping somebody got, and that was Sharky. He got the dogshit kicked outta him by Chris and Brian for ripping them off on some dope. The crazy thing was Sharky was lying in my bed.

I said, "Brian, you know that ain't me, right?"

He said, "We know. You ain't done nothing wrong. We're looking for Sharky."

They yelled, "Get the fuck up, motherfucker!" And Chris just laid into him. He must've hit him fifteen to twenty times. Brian was egging him on. "Give it to him! That motherfucker ripped us off!"

We all just sat there and watched. Everybody hated Sharky.

They didn't beat him unconscious, but I saw him two days later and he was in bad shape. His face looked like one of those deformed tomatoes that's got lumps and bruises all over it.

Sweeny: I didn't bring up my Marine Corps and police background. All they knew was I was from the Northwest, my marriage had fallen apart, and I came to Vegas. That was the extent of the story I told 'em. None of us asked in-depth questions, but we all knew we'd screwed up at some point.

Every day I had a route that I'd walk that took a few hours. That's most of what my day was. Recycling.

There was a guy who'd park behind the Rio and buy the cans. He had a scale in the back of his van. He'd weigh what you had, then pay you in cash. I'd usually have three or four small plastic bags of crushed cans and I'd make ten to fifteen dollars. The other people in the tunnel needed to make more money than I did, because they were into drugs and I was into alcohol. Everyone else's magic number was twenty to twenty-five dollars.

Melinda: We had a Maltese named Blue. He comforted me. For some reason he came around me a lot. I guess he sensed my fear. I always kept him with me and he'd bark if anybody came around.

Jazz, 48, lived in the tunnels off and on from 1996 to 2016 with a small community that included his girlfriend Sharon, Ricky Lee, Jamie, Skip, Zero, and Becky. Born in Thailand, he moved to the States when he was three and grew up mostly in the Southwest. He ended up in Vegas as a teenager and got caught up in the party lifestyle, which eventually resulted in him becoming homeless and moving into the drains: We policed the people that came and went. We had a husband, wife, and kids that got stranded, and we took them in until they could get back on their feet. We had to keep the riffraff out though. We kept it regulated.

People didn't just walk through my camp. I didn't let nobody go through if I didn't know 'em.

Ricky Lee: I didn't need people, but I didn't talk to anybody for a year and it fucked my head up. It made me not able to hold a conversation. It's nice to have people to talk to, but you can't have them taking advantage of you. When someone tries to walk over me I don't just get even; I take everything they have.

This one guy said the tunnel was his and he came at me with a forty-ounce beer bottle. As soon as he swung I ducked and he barely missed my head. I always slept with

RICKY LEE

a knife under my pillow. I rolled, thinking I'm a character in one of the books I'd read, and it was pitch dark and I slashed a couple times. I heard feet running. As soon as I cut on the flashlight I knew I got 'em. He bled all the way outta the tunnel and up to the store. I don't know if he survived, and I don't really care, but he never came back down there again.

For a while I was using echolocation, like a bat. I could walk through the tunnel without a flashlight and not touch anything. I could tell by the echo of my boots if I was close to the wall or something else.

Tex: I've been stabbed. I've been beat. Protecting my territory, standing ground, or just being an innocent victim. The streets and tunnels are hard. They'll do one of two things to you: destroy you or make you stronger. They can turn you into a monster.

The tunnel was cool year-round. It was also secure, and I made it more so because of my MP background and training. I didn't give a fuck either, so if you came down there looking for trouble you were messing with the wrong one. All I wanted was to be left alone. I was there to beat myself up. I was blaming myself for a lotta shit: my mom's death, dropping out of the Army, the death of my ex's stepdad. I wanted to be where I was. I created my own prison.

I could've got off the streets. I didn't become homeless by choice, but I stayed homeless by choice.

Four Finger Mike: At first I flew a sign on Tropicana at the I-15 onramp going south, but that was a battle zone because of this guy Stretch. It was a coveted spot and he'd fight you for it. I got tired of fighting, so I went down to the median in front of In-N-Out and created my own spot there. No one had worked it before. I turned that into a twenty-dollar-an-hour job. I knew not to come before one p.m., and after six it was dead, but between that time I could make a hundred dollars, and some weekends I could come back and make more at night.

I got to know everybody at that intersection. I talked to this one guy every day for a year. He was a construction worker at the CityCenter resort. Never gave me a dollar. We just talked. Then Christmas day he gave me a card that had $200 in it.

This one lady, Jenny, I still talk to till this day. She works the bell desk at TI. I wouldn't say she was a huge tipper, but she gave me about twenty dollars a week and brought food and would take my clothes and wash 'em. She became a good friend.

Stephen: I'd meet up with a street friend of mine when he'd get off work as a painter, and we'd push his cart through UNLV and by McDonald's and KFC. He knew when McDonald's was going to throw away hamburgers. He knew when KFC was going to throw away pot pies. We'd fill up the cart and push it back to the tunnel and feed other homeless people along the way.

I'd hide from my family. I had a sister who'd drive up and down Paradise looking for me, right over the tunnels, just to see if I was alive. I couldn't stand to look in their faces.

Merch: A lot of hustling and getting drugs for people. A middleman. I was going into stores and shoplifting too. Merchandise Mike. Merch. That's what they called me.

Shoplifting was easy. I'd put on a shirt and tie and jacket and have a small duffel bag folded under my arm. I'd take the tags off the items and fill up the bag. Sometimes I'd get a backpack off the rack and fill it up too. Mostly hygiene products: body wash, deodorant, shampoo, toothpaste.

Crack dealers wanted that stuff for themselves and their families. I'd put both bags on the same shoulder, the opposite side of the cashier, and walk out.

One time an undercover Metro officer saw me putting something in the bags, and the manager of the store stopped me on the way out. He wasn't aggressive so I told him, "I don't have anything," and kept walking.

The officer followed me out and across the street. He said, "You got two choices: You can return that stuff or you can wait for the cruisers to come."

I started to walk away and he snatched the bags off my shoulder and repeated what he'd said. I dropped the bags and kept walking. I knew I wasn't gonna win that battle.

I only had thirteen shoplifting convictions in Vegas. After fifteen years of doing it two or three times a day in places like Walgreens, Albertsons, Smith's, and CVS, that's not bad. I probably stole close to $30,000 of merchandise a year.

Cyndi: Me and Rick would dumpster-dive behind Burlington and find broken jewelry. I'd fix it and sell it on the street. We wanted to try to earn the money.

TK, 34, lived in the tunnels off and on from 2002 to 2013. He is a friend of Rick and Cyndi's and occasionally lived with them in a drain near Tropicana and Eastern avenues. For several years he was a fixture at that intersection, where he panhandled with his dog Spanger: Somebody abandoned a dog—a blue-nose pit bull and black lab mix— and my friend found him when he was five months old. His name was originally Rampage. When I looked at him I said, "Spanger," which means spare changer or someone who asks for change.

My friend gave me a white pair of Locs sunglasses, and I was playing around and put them on the dog and he didn't shake 'em off. He always grabbed the skateboard. He loved carrying it in his mouth. I was like, Cool! Let's hit the corner!

Our main spot was Trop and Eastern. That's where we started. We got famous at Trop and Pecos when we made the morning paper. We'd go to Flamingo and Eastern too, depending on the weather and how much energy we had.

Eventually I built a cart and I'd push him around in it. In the summer I'd put fans and misters on it 'cause I have to take care of my dog.

The way to make money is to get people's attention. All I had to do is get 'em to look. One way to do that is with music. I had a boombox. My sign was on the cart. It didn't say I was homeless, but it hinted at it: "Unemployed and hungry."

I did this from 2008 to 2013 or 2014 and easily made two grand a month. Spanger and I fed a lot of homeless people in the area.

Zero: My best lick was with this guy Larry. It was two in the morning and we were walking through the MGM using it as a shortcut. The guy in front of us steps over something and keeps walking. I pick it up.

Larry said, "What's that?"

"A big wad of money." It had a rubber band around it and it was very thick.

My adrenaline was surging and we beelined to Larry's room. He was six-foot-three and 300 pounds and he was walking faster than me. We got to the room and I pulled out the wad. He took the rubber band off and started counting: 100, 200, 300 . . . 800, 900, 1,000. He finally stopped at $3,600.

We split the money. If you're partnering with somebody you split everything. I went and played poker and got crack and weed and was up for the next two days, then fell asleep for a day in all my clothes. Gary got $200 of crack, then called this hooker he knew and went to the San Remo and got a room for four days, smoking and having sex.

I could get stuck in a casino for days. I'd find fifty dollars in a slot machine and play it up to $200, then cash out and go play bingo and make two hundred more. Then I could go to the blackjack table and lose it all in fifteen minutes.

One day I was in a casino from dayshift to dayshift. I was talking to the security guard, and the next day when he came to work I was playing the same machine and wearing the same clothes. He did a double take. Probably had a déjà-vu moment.

Finally he said, "You ever gonna go home?"

"Why would I do that?" I said.

He just smiled and walked off.

Ned: I'm a pretty good marketer, so it was easy for me to pick a niche and take it underground and build contacts that provided me with the best club passes, pool passes, and wristbands. I started with this massive duffel bag, then downsized to a man purse with the proper materials and pitch. You had to know how to work a crowd. That's what you looked for: big groups of guys or girls or a nice-looking couple. You'd profile and make your pitch, then ask questions, just like when I was selling Beemers.

"Why are you in Vegas? Are you married? How hard do you wanna party?" Some people caught that reference and would pull me aside.

If I saw a group of bachelorettes coming toward me I'd look in my satchel and arrange a few things in it. I read the *Las Vegas Weekly* and knew who was at what club—if LAX had, say, Tiësto or Kim Kardashian. If the girls had penis straws in their mouths maybe they wanted to go to a male review: Chippendales or Thunder from Down Under. I'd get them two-for-one passes or a free limo ride and pitch them on what it normally costs.

"It's forty dollars a head at the door, but with these passes I can get you complimentary limo service and into the club and a ride back to your hotel for free. The passes are also free. We work on gratuities. Since there's six of you, at forty dollars a head I'm saving you $240. Ten bucks apiece would be nice, and I'll call the limo for you now."

In three minutes I'd make sixty dollars, and I did it the right way. Called the limo, called the promoter, told the club to expect them. I was legit.

There were violent moments and prosperous ones. Worrying about Dee's safety because she's putting herself out there in a way that may be threatening to others, and those people may retaliate. And these weren't just random people. They were thugs who didn't give a shit, trash who'd stab or shoot you without a second thought. Harm was done. Guns came into play. I never shot a gun, but I used knives to protect us. I'm pretty good at close-quarter confrontation.

It's shameful to be talking about this, but we lived it and we prepared as much as possible. Knives in every pocket, brass knuckles, a rock or roll of quarters as a fist pack. There were some nail-biting times. You had these little scabby fucks who wanted to rob you for whatever you had. It was mental rape more than anything else. Brain damage.

It's frightening what people do to each other at that level.

Barry: It was similar to prison in some ways. A small space. Blank walls, then you put up pictures. The difference was in the tunnels you had the freedom to come and go as you chose. Also, in prison, you got light 24/7.

I preferred the tunnels to prison 'cause at least I could come and go as I pleased.

Jamie: Kregg and Zero showed me how to hustle the casinos. They were advantage players and card cheats and credit hustlers. Kregg's a special guy. He talks with his hands and can have your attention over here and take your wallet out of your pocket without you even knowing it. He's that good. They showed me how matchplays work. That's the only guaranteed bet in Vegas. It takes two people to do it and two coupons, but it can't miss.

Zero and I would hit the craps tables at Planet Hollywood, which had fifty-dollar matchplays on all three shifts. We'd go to a table and wait for a new shooter. He or she's either going to crap out or catch a point, and we'd cover both sides of the bet. The dealers knew what we were doing when they saw the coupons come out. One's a guaranteed winner, one's a guaranteed loser, but since they were matching your money it was actually a $100 bet. You'd win a hundred and lose fifty, so you made fifty dollars.

We'd also get players-club cards and put them in the dollar Wheel of Fortune slot machines, and tourists would play the machines for hours and not realize they were putting points on our card. They had no idea the card was in the machine. Most of these people had never seen a slot machine in their life. We'd use the points to gamble or get food.

I had a pocketful of money and a pocketful of dope. That's how we lived. We didn't need anything else.

SKY HIGH

As shown in the last chapter, the Las Vegas storm drains can be cruel and unforgiving. Addiction is rampant. Theft and assault are commonplace. In an instant, a wall of water can wipe out months of work, carrying away one's home and any sliver of hope.

But the chapter also included rays of light amid the darkness: camaraderie, tranquility, ingenuity, decorum, humanity, love. Small victories that had a large impact. Poetry among the prosaic daily grind of hustle, score, hustle, score, hustle, score.

These moments humanize the tunnel residents and help normalize the experience, and I wanted the interviewees to expound on them. Hence the two questions that guided this chapter: What was your happiest moment in the drains? Do you have any fond memories of that time?

Tommy: Finding a briefcase after a rain. It had washed into the tunnel. I opened it and there were eight $100 bills in it. There was some paperwork and stuff too, but I didn't bother to look at it. Let's party! That's all I was thinking.

I got a weekly and went at it hard. Big chunks of crack, a bag of weed, lots of booze. I didn't pay for alcohol often because my friends would boost it, but I made an exception this time.

Iron: The crew from MTV's *The Buried Life* came down to the spot. The idea of the show was if you knew you were gonna die in forty-eight hours what would you do. I told 'em, "I'd wanna meet my granddaughter and spend some time with my daughter."

They set it all up. Drove me to Missouri, where my daughter was living. Put me up in a nice hotel. When I showed up at her front door I was scared to death. Didn't know if she was going to hug or punch me. It'd been ten years since I'd seen her.

She hugged me and we cried and I got to meet my granddaughter and spend a few days with 'em.

I didn't know anything about *The Buried Life*. Didn't really find out what it was till later. I thought it was just some little show. No big deal. Come to find out it was *really* popular. For a while I couldn't walk down the street without someone sticking their head out the window and yelling, "*The Buried Life!*"

Cyndi: During the holidays I always wanted to get smashed. I couldn't stand the way I felt—the loneliness, guilt, and despair. One Thanksgiving I told Rick, "Let's go to the casino and gamble and drink." I wanted to cover up the negative feelings I was having. Then a few people with the Shine a Light program came into the tunnel with Thanksgiving dinner. That touched my heart and changed the way I felt about the holidays.

Phil: I was hitting the pipe behind a dumpster and a cop drove by, so I ducked and threw my shit into the dumpster. I had to go in and get it, and when I did it was like Christmas: full of candy bars and pastries.

I got my crack situation handled, then I walked to the tunnel and told everyone what was going on. We hit that dumpster like there was no tomorrow. People I didn't even know showed up.

Turns out there was plenty to go around in that dumpster on a regular basis.

I was with this guy we called Stupid Steve and it was during the World Series of Poker. This tourist was fucked up on a machine at the Rio, lifting his shirt over his head, and there were a bunch of twenty- and fifty-dollar bills under his seat. Steve wanted to swoop in right away, but I said, "Hold tight."

I circled around and sat at the machine next to the guy and started dragging the money with my foot. I had to bend over three times to pick it all up. We came out of there with $2,800.

We go down to the hole and I break everybody off like I'm some sorta player. I go do my laundry at Auntie M's market and I fuck around on a machine there and hit a royal for $1,000.

Me and Steve were on a run the whole night. We said we need to stay together. We got the luck. And we ended up hitting a five-team parlay at the Palms.

The morning came and the dope man wasn't ready yet, and I ended up winning another $600 on a machine. I had $3,500 in my pocket.

I'd be a millionaire if I held onto all the money I found and won while living in the tunnels.

Four Finger Mike: Going to used bookstores or Savers or Goodwill. I like to read: Clancy, Ludlum, W. E. B. Griffin, Grisham. I didn't wanna get high all the time. I got up and read the paper every day, and there were weeks where all I did was sit around and read books and newspapers.

One Shoe Sue: There are a few friends I remember fondly. One was Misti. She had blonde hair and was short and spoke with a British accent. We'd go to the Wild Wild West and gamble. If we had a stretch of good luck, maybe we could get a room for a few days and take a shower. That was the best you could hope for down there.

Pretty Boy Steve: I really have to think about that. I guess just finding out who me and Kat were. I remember everybody making smart comments about us—they're always together and all they ever do is laugh. That's a bad thing?

We fell in love in that tunnel.

You'd bring in a piece of furniture and everybody's eyes got big.

"How'd you get that down here?"

"I carried it on my back."

Just kidding. Shopping carts, which are everywhere in Vegas. We'd put the furniture on top of a cart and wheel it down the street. It's one of those times you gotta say to yourself, I don't care what anyone thinks. We need this to live more comfortably.

Becky: Me and Zero had tons of good times in the casinos. Popping tickets and running. Fighting other hustlers for the right machine. Getting drunk as hell and meeting interesting people from all over the world.

But we didn't have much fun in the tunnels. I cried a lot down there because I missed my daughter and I was disappointed in what I was doing with my life. I couldn't

EASY E

believe I'd stooped so low. Then I'd shoot up meth to try to mask the pain. As long as I was high down there I was okay.

Easy E: The only fond memory I have is when I left the tunnels.

You can sugarcoat a turd and make it edible, but nah, dude, there was nothing fun about it. Sure, I had some laughs and did a lot of crazy shit with interesting people. I got funny stories of dealing with cops and security guards and bullshitting my way out of all types of situations. I met people I'm going to be friends with for life, some that I consider family.

But stealing that money from my dad and driving to Las Vegas was the biggest mistake of my life. I ain't ever told anyone this: The day I left New York was my parents' anniversary. They went out to dinner with their friends who had the same anniversary, and I stole from them and took off without saying a word.

Shaggy: There was a guy down there I didn't get along with. Damien. In fact, we fought several times. But when it really came down to it we looked out for each other. There were a few instances when he went out of his way to make sure my camp was safe, and he brought me a bag of stuff one day and said, "Bro, I found this in a camp down the way and I know it's yours." Sure as shit it was all my stuff that had gone missing.

To this day if I were to see him on the streets there'd be bad blood, but those moments were nice. I felt like I was part of a family.

It rained and our beds flipped and dammed the water. We were collecting our stuff, thinking the worst was over. Then we heard the dam break. Leah, who has since passed away, was sitting on the bed eating peanut butter outta the jar. Her boyfriend said, "Fuck the peanut butter! We gotta go!"

It was just like a movie. We were running and the water and all the debris was right behind us. We got outta the tunnel, and carts and bikes and mattresses flew right by us. We stood on top of the bank laughing, watching it all pass by.

Rick: There was a lot of good times actually. Me and Cyndi were able to help other people and we felt like we were of some use. There was always people out there that were worse off than we were, and it felt good to help them. It gave us purpose.

We'd go on what we called "blue walks." We'd check all the areas where we knew our heroin-addict friends would go to shoot up. We called 'em "blue walks" because when someone overdoses they tend to turn blue.

Sometimes we'd buy people food with our food stamps. We'd hit dumpsters and have extras handy. When we couldn't buy or find food I'd steal it. We didn't have a choice.

We had four beds, two couches, and a loveseat. One night during the winter, when we went to bed, it was just me and Cyndi. When we woke up the next morning there were eleven other people there.

Stephen: There were no good times. You're hiding from your family, trying to get as high as you can so you forget everything. I remember walking down the street thinking, Just step in front of the next fast-moving truck. Get it over with.

Fear, pain, and loneliness is all that's down there. Even when I was with that one girl I liked, the one who disappeared for a year and a half, it was fun for only an hour or two and then you wanted more. More drinks, more drugs, more money. More, more, more. You were constantly in need of something.

Ricky Lee: When I got a job with the Department of Transportation. I was cleaning the bridges and elevators and escalators on the Strip. It was full time.

Also, every now and then, we'd have barbecues in the tunnels. Jazz would steal the food. We'd build a makeshift grill. Of course alcohol was served. It was usually me, Ervin, Red, Butch, and Jazz. The cops would come and tell us to keep the noise and smoke down. We'd have a good time, especially on the Fourth of July.

Kat: Blue, the Maltese. He took to the tunnel like he was born in it. He loved it. He'd go from camp to camp each morning and everybody would give him a treat. He really brought us together.

I found him at a bus stop. It was raining and I was taking the bus home. He came up to me shivering. I said, "Come on. I'll keep you warm."

We tried to find his owners. We searched the papers and even put an ad in the free weeklies. When no one responded he became ours. We all took care of him.

Maddie: This is how I found out Knyck liked me:

His friend Damage asked me for a massage because he was sore from walking all day. I said, "No problem."

I was giving him a massage and Knyck got up and walked off. He came back twenty minutes later and walked right past me and went and sat on the couch. I stopped what I was doing and walked over and asked what's wrong.

He didn't answer, but I could tell what it was. He didn't like that I gave his friend a massage. Knyck and I got together after that, then three days later he said, "I love you."

I was underage at the time, but I was mature, and I've never gotten along with people my age, especially guys. Knyck was older and unique. I liked his mind. He was the first guy I met that treated me right, who was against yelling and violence and was loyal.

Knyck: I'd never hooked up with a girl that young. I was twenty-six and she was fifteen when we got drunk one night and had sex. It just happened. The next day I was like, If I say we can't do this I'm an asshole and if I say it's okay I'm a perv. I was stuck in a weird place.

Jodie: Sitting in lounge chairs with Eddie outside the tunnel, drinking beer and shooting the shit and shooting at cans with a BB gun we'd found in a dumpster.

Sweeny: Phil had "The Round Table"—a big, round table he'd found on the streets—and we'd sit there and talk sports. He's a Boston fan. I root for Seattle. He usually had good weed too. If we weren't doing anything better we'd sit at the table with the light coming through the grate and look at sports-betting sheets and smoke weed. Easy E was usually there. We'd pool what little money we had and place five- and ten-dollar sports bets.

I got along with Phil, which seems kinda weird. I don't think we would've hung out under any other circumstances.

Melinda: The times I got to talk with Kat. Having another woman down there made me feel safe. Her and Steve had their spot decorated really nice, and I'd ask her how I could make me and Manny's camp nicer. We'd talk about our children and how much we loved and missed them. It felt good to talk to somebody because, at times, I felt like I didn't have anybody to talk to.

Easy E had a good heart too. And Phil. Everyone down there had their own story. Kat had lost custody of her son. Phil lost his father. My dad abandoned me, and my mom was gone a lot. We'd drink and talk about it all. Pity parties, I guess, but it was comforting, and after a while we got to know and trust each other.

It seems like God made us meet down there for some reason, but I don't know why.

Jamie: Every day there was something going on. It was such a casually intense lifestyle—that'd be one way to describe it. You're on the edge of humanity. There's nowhere lower. It's the basement of rock bottom, but there was a lot of camaraderie between us. We looked out for each other.

Zero: I never had problems at the Venetian. I was lucky. They've tackled people on the sidewalk and dragged 'em back into the casino. They've got facial recognition. Sometimes I'd walk in and within a minute five guards were coming at me. I'd just turn around and leave.

I took Jamie in there one night. We had these counterfeit coupons and one was for a twenty-five-dollar free play on your players card. We played a few of the coupons, won a few bucks, ordered some beers. I was thinking about playing another one when four security guards and two suits with radios approached.

This one guard said to me, "Excuse me, sir. Do you have an ID?"

I said, "Of course. Isn't it required by law?" He nodded and I said, "Thanks for asking."

"Can I see it?" he said.

"Why?"

"I need to see it, sir."

"Can I see yours?"

"My badge is right here." He pointed to his chest.

"No. Your driver's license. If you wanna see my name and address and date of birth it's only right that I get to see yours."

"Sir, let me see your ID."

It was becoming a spectacle. I was talking really loud and tourists were stopping and looking.

Finally, I took out my wallet and handed him this UFO driver's license that I boosted from a gift shop. It had a picture of a green alien whose name was A. Leon.

He looked at it a while, then said, "I need a valid driver's license, sir."

"Can't you read? This license is valid in thirteen galaxies!"

The suits were cracking up, Jamie was laughing his ass off, and the guard looked like he was about to pop. His face was red.

He finally gave the ID back to me, and Jamie and I walked off laughing.

I'd take a seven iron and golf balls and walk out into the desert. I'd spot something—a big bush or debris—and make it my hole and give it a par, say three or four strokes. That was my stress relief. Pounding balls into the sunset.

I'd hike a couple miles out and think about not coming back. Just walking off into the sunset with a seven iron slung over my shoulder.

ROCK BOTTOM

After asking the interviewees about their happiest moment in the drains, I felt compelled to inquire about their darkest memory. What was your lowest point down there? When did you hit rock bottom?

The responses were devastating and, in some cases, unfathomable: vicious beatings, stabbings, shootings, life-threatening infections and diseases, raging fires, biblical floods. Some of the moments were so traumatic they forced the interviewees to re-evaluate their lives entirely. All leading up to the ultimate tunnel tragedy.

Melinda: When I got this scar.

Manny choked me until my eyes popped out. The only thing that made him stop was I begged him to tell my children that I love them, because I thought I was going to die. Tell them I'm sorry for everything and I miss them so much.

He let go and threw me against the wall. When I woke up, Kat was stitching a cut above my eye. I could hear Manny crying and saying, "Is she dead? What should I do?"

They didn't call an ambulance; they had addictions and didn't want to get in trouble. For days they made me lay there. Manny, of course, was saying he's sorry and trying to calm me down because he was afraid I was going to snitch and he'd go back to prison.

When we broke up several years later the last thing he told me was, "You'll never forget me because every time you look in the mirror you'll see that scar."

Kat: Steve and I came home and discovered a trail of blood. There was blood on our bed, on the floor, everywhere. Manny had thrown Melinda against the wall. She's lucky to be alive.

Manny told us, "I'm useless! Call the police!" He started crying. He can turn on the tears like a light switch.

I asked Melinda what she wanted to do and she said, "Stop bleeding."

Steve went to the store and got a bag of ice, which helped. I told her she needed stitches, she needed to go to the hospital, but she refused. She didn't want Manny to get in trouble.

Manny: Me and Melinda had some ugly fights. We nitpicked each other and she knew exactly where to hit me to hurt me, and she did it on a regular basis.

But the one I'll always remember is tipping the bed. "Get up!" I told her. "Let's go! I have money."

I tipped the mattress over and she fell off. Everyone thinks I popped her or threw her against the wall, but I just tilted the bed and she hit the wall.

Jamie: The fire.

These dealers owed me and Kregg money for some stolen Tommy Bahama shirts. I ain't 100 percent sure who set the fire, but it started at my camp. I woke up to searing heat, blinding smoke, and barely enough air for one gasp to haul ass outta there. An aerosol can blew up. That's what brought me to. I'd been awake for a week gambling and doing meth.

My mattress was in a completely different position than when I went to sleep. I noticed that even before I gasped for air. All I could do was run. I ran downstream 'cause I could gauge where I was; that's usually the way I went in and out. Zero and Becky and Kregg went upstream, which was the shortest route. I was knocking stuff over and woke up Skip and Manny and Melinda, who'd just moved down there from a tunnel by the Rio. I left all my money, drugs, clothes. I made it to the bottom end and turned and went in the other tunnel and told Ricky Lee what happened. He gave me a blanket and said, "Just chill here, man. It's all good."

I think one of the guys in the tunnels started the fire. One of 'em was the kinda person who'd give you the shirt off his back, then stab you in the back through that shirt. He's the main suspect.

I'd started calling the dealers, telling 'em, "Hey, motherfucker! You owe me money!" Threatening them. I was a different person when I was on dope. I was a dangerous guy. I was fixin' to be a big problem.

Either one of the people in the tunnels took it upon himself to set my camp on fire and try to kill me, or one of the dealers paid him to do it.

Skip, 60, is an accomplished drummer who lived in the drains off and on for two years. Originally from Euclid, Ohio, he moved to California in his thirties. After spending some time in Oregon, he caught a Greyhound bus to Las Vegas, where he hoped to find work as a musician. He held a variety of jobs—cook, casino promoter, pedicab driver—

before falling on hard times and landing in the tunnels: I heard someone yell, "Help!"

I said, "Who's that?"

"It's Jamie! Where are you? Keep talking!" He didn't know which way was which.

I smelled the smoke, and Jamie got to me and he looked like Freddy Krueger. The heat was so intense it almost set my clothes on fire from 200 feet away. I ran out the tunnel and looked up at the smoke. It was thick going across the Strip and into the airport.

He fell asleep with a cigarette. I went back in the tunnel the next day and could see his handprint with it. I said, "Good job, motherfucker!" There was ashes everywhere.

He goes, "I'm freezing. I don't have nothin'."

"I don't give a fuck." All our shit was there, but it was coated with soot, and I ended up having to clean it.

I was depressed about being in the tunnels and I had someone stick a needle in my arm. He missed the vein.

A couple days later I was on the bus and I felt like I was dying. A horrible headache. The pain was unbelievable. I was nauseous. Like a really bad hangover. I couldn't go any farther. I got off and was lying there at the bus stop. I didn't know what was wrong. Do I have food poisoning?

I made it back to the tunnel, but I didn't get better. Sharon and this guy Luis kept bringing me food and water. Luis said, "It stinks in here." I was pissing myself because I couldn't get up to use the bathroom.

Sharon finally said, "You're going to the hospital!"

The last thing I remember was her bringing me some pizza. When I came to I was in my underwear and Dale Earnhardt sweatshirt, and four doctors were saying they were gonna have to cut off my arm.

The doctors told me it was an abscess and the infection was feeding on my bicep tissue. It deteriorated everything at a fast pace. My arm was sore and I couldn't lift it. My kidneys hurt. A nurse said, "His blood sugar is 500!"

My arm was black. Gangrene. The stench was terrible. The doctors repeated, "We don't think we can save it. We have to cut it off."

"Please try to save it! Do whatever you can!" I was praying. I told God, "I'm done with the tunnels and drugs. No more. Just get this infection outta my body."

The doctors wound-packed the abscess and went in and sucked the infection out. It'd gotten into my bloodstream. My kidneys failed. They removed my bottom biceps muscle. I had two blood transfusions, three operations. I was in the hospital for six weeks. But they saved my arm. A medical miracle. Ninety-nine percent of the people who have that infection lose their arm.

Ned: After thirteen years together Dee and I drifted apart. We stopped making love because I knew she was sharing needles. She started seeing someone else. It broke my heart.

There was no more love. We were just looking out for each other, and it became apparent that I was giving too much of myself away. I wanted to understand the pain she went through with her father. I didn't understand it, I guess, but I loved her enough to give a shit and to try to get a glimpse of it. Maybe I can help her heal, I thought, but I was losing myself and my ethics in the process, and I started numbing my own pain more and more.

One Shoe Sue: There was a time I'd do anything to get two or three dollars. I wasn't a girl who shot for big bucks. I was a Four Loko or Mad Dog 20/20 girl. That's all I was trying to get.

It was pitiful. I was in my forties and lying about my age and name. Stealing and turning tricks, and not very good at either of 'em. I got arrested eleven times for prostitution alone.

I was within two miles of my family home. I knew that my mom had cancer and that Shaggy and my younger son were close by. I'd see my brother's truck drive past. You wear a mask. Matted hair, dirty underwear. I was so filthy from living down there, and I didn't even care.

Easy E: I did one purse-snatch on an old woman. Three hundred bucks. Ripped it right off her shoulder in front of the Gold Coast casino.

Maddie: I was hanging out with one of my girlfriends and she noticed that my eyelids were starting to turn yellow. She said that means your liver's not good. That's when I started to realize how bad the drinking had gotten. I was chugging a half-gallon to a gallon every day. Anything I could get my hands on. I was a tequila girl, but you don't have a choice when you're homeless. You drink what you got.

I started to wean myself off the alcohol, but switched to heroin. I thought that was better because I was close to killing myself drinking.

Shaggy: I'd resolved that this was it. I was going to die in the tunnels with a needle in my arm. I was accepting of that. I didn't care.

Around that same time my girlfriend pulled a knife on me because I was dopesick and didn't want to get any more drugs. I was fed up with how we were living. She'd only been down there six or seven months. I was coming up on three years.

Iron: I hit rock bottom once a week. Just the way I was living. I knew I could do better. I knew I was doing wrong, but I did it anyway. Why? I still don't have the answer to that question.

Rick: Me and Cyndi were staying in the tunnel and TK was staying in a dumpster area nearby. We weren't feeling good and we walked to his spot to get some weed from him. While we were there Cyndi and I got violently ill. We couldn't even walk so we spent the night there.

Somebody showed up the next morning and said the county was at the tunnel throwing our stuff away. I limped down there. Had to stop and relieve myself because I almost shit my pants, and I stepped in someone else's shit on the way.

When I got there the workers were like, "Who are you?"

I had to explain who I was with a finger in my mouth and turning to the side to puke. "This is my stuff," I said. "It's everything me and my wife own."

I asked them if I could at least grab my wife's purse so she has her ID. Can I grab a coat? Anything?

They said you can't have nothing. A vice officer was there. He said, "They've told you many times you need to be outta here. Walk away now or I'm taking you to jail!"

I came back later and it turned out the workers were cool. They'd left a women's coat, a men's coat, and one backpack with some clothes in it. So there we were with nothing but two coats and a backpack and too sick to go look for anything else.

Occasionally I was able to borrow some tools and do honest work, but just enough to get Cyndi and I some food or meth or alcohol to help numb the pain. I could never seem to get up enough money to get us out of there, and the few times I did walk out with some money in my pocket, I couldn't make it past the first liquor store or drug dealer—and there's lots of both of those on every block in Las Vegas.

But one time I really thought we were gonna make it out. A guy offered me a job as a maintenance man and gave me room, board, and wage. I worked for him for five weeks and he only paid me a scooter and $100, and we were living in a house that was foreclosed on and the power was turned on illegally and we could go to jail at any time.

I said, "Hey, can you pay me for my work?"

He said, "I break into foreclosed homes and change the locks and rent 'em to people. If you help me I'll cut you in on the money."

I told him I couldn't do that, and Cyndi and I went back to the tunnel. At that point we gave up hope of ever getting out.

Tex: I got shot at because I was a vet panhandling on the street. If the guy hadn't been drunk he would've killed me.

I had my sign. I was walking up the off-ramp. It was three in the morning. I seen him roll his window down. Hell yeah. I'm gonna go to McDonald's in a couple hours and get me a sausage McMuffin. I couldn't afford the egg McMuffin.

I seen him reach into his center console. I didn't care if it was change. I was blessed with whatever you gave me, fifteen cents or fifteen dollars. I seen panhandlers say, "If you can't give me five bucks don't even bother." I wasn't like that. If they gave me food that made it easier. I wouldn't have to walk to McDonald's. I could eat right there on the corner.

I kept my distance from him. I respected people's privacy and didn't crowd 'em. But instead of change he pulls out a gun. I'm laughing. I'm like, It's fake. He locks and loads it. Shit, it's real! It caught me off guard and I just stood there. I couldn't move.

He points it at me and pulls the trigger. Scared me so bad I still didn't move. I was frozen.

The bullet shattered his windshield. It hit near the metal doorframe and spiderwebbed that whole side.

The light turns green and he nonchalantly drives off like nothing happened, so I nonchalantly pull out my cell phone and call 911. "Shut up and take down this license plate before I forget it!"

It was freezing cold one Christmas and I was starving. A car was at the light and the driver whistled for me to come over and he had a Subway sandwich in his hand. I got about halfway to the car and the dude unwraps the sandwich, takes a bite of it, and spits it at me and says, "Merry fucking Christmas!" Then he drives off.

TEX

I've been hit with eggs and oranges. I've never personally had piss thrown on me, but I watched a friend of mine get hit with it. That's another reason I kept my distance from vehicles. Not just to protect them but to protect me, because if you throw piss on me and I get my hands on you I'm going to jail for a long time.

Me and this guy didn't get along. He didn't like me and I didn't like him. I don't know if he was jealous of me or what. Seemed like he was. I always did better than he did panhandling on the corner.

I had a hook up at Capriotti's and they gave me six subs and I offered his girl one. He come up to me and said, "Don't ever talk to my girl again!"

I said, "Fuck you! I'll talk to whoever I want to! It's a free country!"

I walked to the off-ramp at I-15 and Sahara and was making money. He was in the center of Sahara. I was waiting for him to come off because there was more traffic there. He got on his bike to leave and I got on my bike to go to the center and he turned and come toward me. He started running his mouth and told me to get off my bike.

I was like, Hell yeah. This motherfucker don't have no chain, he ain't got no knife, he ain't got no gun. I'm finally gonna get to whoop his ass. I knew if he wasn't strapped I was going to beat his ass and I wanted to. I had it in for him. He'd fucked with me too much.

I got off my bike and we started swinging. I hit him good. I'm a southpaw. I'm a little slow, but if I connect I'm gonna hurt you. I knocked him smooth off his feet and he fell down into the middle of Sahara. I was fixin' to go stomp his head into the asphalt. I was gonna kill him. I looked down and saw the blade in his hand and he was already up off the ground before I could move. Then I saw blood dripping and I could feel the pain.

The motherfucker stabbed me! Twice in my arm and once in my lower back, and I didn't even know it! I got back on my bike and took off.

I got thirteen stitches—seven in my arm, six in my back. If he would've stabbed a quarter-inch lower in my back he would've killed me. He would've hit a major artery and I would've bled to death.

Tommy: Not being able to light a cigarette in the morning. Someone else would have to light it for me. I'd have the shakes so bad until I had a few shots of booze.

Vegas Dee: It was time for me to go. I knew I'd never see Ned again. It was time to say goodbye to everyone and everything.

I was in the middle of a court case and was gonna go to jail. Also, my neck was messed up. It started swelling. I shot up and missed the vein and almost died. I was in deep and there wasn't enough dope to make me feel better.

It was cold and we had makeshift walls up and they couldn't keep the wind out. The place had gone to pot and really bad people started coming down. I looked at Ned and said, "I'm outta here."

I didn't wanna leave. It was all I'd known for the past two years. But I was killing myself.

My mom sent a cab for me and got me a room and flew in the next day, then she rented a car and came and got me. We left Las Vegas that morning. I was so sick. I'd told her when she sees me she's gonna freak out. "No, honey, I won't." She was so good, but I know she was freaked out because my neck was completely swollen and pus was oozing out of it.

I said, "Don't get pulled over, Mom. I'm wanted by the police."

Ande: July 2014. Another hot day. I was in the tunnel wearing a tank top and I felt a lump the size of an apricot pit on my right breast. I thought, This is not good. What am I gonna do?

I'd gotten the application for Medicaid when I signed up for food stamps, so I set up a doctor's appointment—the earliest one was in October—and figured out the bus route and how to get there. The doctor said this is definitely not good and he referred me to another doctor, who didn't have an opening till March. She did a mammogram and when the results came in she called me. I was sleeping in the tunnel. "Just wanted to let you know we found cancer and we're gonna take care of you from head to toe. There's nothing to worry about."

She said she couldn't give me chemotherapy because I lived in a tunnel; you'll die of a disease down there. She said, "We have this other treatment. It's two shots in the butt."

That's all they could do.

The county came down twice, once right after I'd been diagnosed with cancer. I was at work, holding up a sign for a loan company. One of my friends drove by the tunnel and saw what was going on and called me. I raced back there and six trucks and two bulldozers were clearing everything out.

I'd posted notes saying, "Diagnosed with Cancer. Please Don't Take My Stuff." They also had my phone number on 'em. I wrote those notes to transients who might steal from me while I wasn't there. That happened a lot, but they didn't steal everything; they couldn't carry it all. The county cleared me out. Threw away all my vitamins, medicine, and brand-new clothes I got for the doctors' appointments.

"Why didn't you call me?" I asked 'em, and they totally blew me off. Everyone there was telling 'em to at least let me get my meds from the back of the truck. They just laughed and went and had lunch at Subway.

Jazz: The night before I came in kinda late. I brought back some groceries. My girlfriend Sharon and I were just chilling, watching music videos on her phone and talking.

It had rained that day so I stayed up all night to make sure it didn't rain again. I remember walking outside in the morning and seeing clear skies. I thought everything was good and I went to sleep. When I woke up I heard somebody screaming and Sharon screaming too. A foot of water had hit us in our sleep.

We'd done this a hundred times. We know what we have to do—gather all our things in shopping carts and roll them outside to the channel and lock 'em to a tow chain—but I'm trying to grab her purse and our phones. The water comes in waves. It's a rush. And when the second wave hit it was over our knees.

I told her to get out, to get up the embankment.

A third wave came and hit me in the chest. I'm six feet tall. Sharon's five-two and she got washed away in the open channel. I jumped in after her. When I caught up to her I tried to pick her up, but couldn't. The water was too strong. In twenty years in the tunnel I'd never seen anything like this.

We came to the first rebar ladder and I told her I'm gonna try to grab it. We were moving thirty miles an hour. I grabbed the ladder and it almost ripped my arm off.

As we were going around a corner I saw some people we knew standing on the bank. I wanted them to throw us a lifeline, but there was nothing they could do. They just screamed, "Oh my God!"

We hit another turn and the water washed us all the way up to the top of the bank. I could almost grab the fence. The channel was fifteen feet tall.

The whole time I'm telling her what we're gonna do. Our last chance of getting out was a ramp. I told her to swim for it. I said, "When we get to the ramp roll onto it!"

I let go of her and rolled onto the ramp, but she kept going.

The water washed me back into the current. She was twenty-five yards ahead of me and she turned around and looked at me. I tried to swim toward her, but I couldn't catch up. She was moving so fast.

At the end of the channel there's a grate that collects the debris before the wash goes underground again. When we hit the grate, the water was so strong it pushed me and her to the top of it. There was all kinds of debris hitting us— shopping carts, chairs, anything you can think of—and we got separated.

When I found her she was on her back with her leg bent. I asked her what's wrong and she said her leg was caught. I reached down and pulled on her leg. She screamed. Something was wrapped around it.

I didn't know what do to. I didn't have a knife to cut whatever was wrapped around her leg. The water had ripped the clothes off my body. I was getting sliced by debris.

I yanked on her leg a couple more times, then a shopping cart hit her and flipped on top of her like a lid. I couldn't get the cart off her. I was doing everything I could, but I couldn't get it off her, man!

The water above the grate started rising. In a matter of seconds it was overflowing the wash and into the streets. Sharon was underneath it.

Here came another friend of ours from the tunnel. He was floating by with this look in his eyes like he was lost. I grabbed his arm and pulled him out and told him, "Sharon's in there, bro!"

I started screaming for help because there's an apartment complex nearby. People were standing there looking, but nobody was helping.

When Fire & Rescue showed up she'd been underwater for six or seven minutes. I'm telling 'em where she's at and how long she's been there. I'm screaming at the top of my lungs.

They put me in an ambulance and took me to Valley Hospital. On the way I asked 'em, "What's Sharon's status? What's happening?"

They said, "We got a report of a man and woman who got rescued."

I'm thinking, All right. Maybe they got her out and brought her back to life.

I got to the hospital and it was a blur after that. When I checked out they gave me a bus pass and I went back to the neighborhood and ran into Sharon's ex-husband at McDonald's. He was trying to find out if she was okay. I told him what happened and he said, "Let's go find her!" It was four in the morning, twelve hours after we got washed away.

Digging through the debris looking for Sharon, my hands were all cut up. I couldn't dig no more. I needed a rake or shovel or something. The debris could've filled a dump truck.

I went back to our camp and everything was gone. Our whole house. With that much force nothing could've survived.

Later that morning I walked back to the scene with some friends and we saw the coroner's office, Fire & Rescue, and police. I told 'em who I was and wrote a statement. The coroner asked me what Sharon was wearing. I described her Ed Hardy T-shirt and she told me they found her.

ROAD TO REDEMPTION PART I

In November 2019, Las Vegas Mayor Carolyn Goodman and the City Council created international news by making it illegal for people to sleep on the streets when shelter beds are available. The law is eerily similar to many that were passed by her husband and predecessor, Oscar Goodman, who closed parks and led the criminalization of public feedings. The former Mob attorney also proposed shipping the homeless to an abandoned prison outside of the city, an idea his wife has revitalized (in a slightly altered form).

Oscar Goodman, who served from 1999 to 2011, often said that people on the streets want to be homeless. His wife shares this belief, as do a lot of Las Vegans and Americans. However, my experience with the Shine a Light outreach program suggests it's not entirely accurate.

No one, of course, grows up wanting to be homeless. But once on the streets, some choose to remain there because they enjoy the freedom, they don't want to give up the drugs or alcohol, they lack self-esteem, or for some other reason. As Tex explained in the "Life Below" chapter, he didn't become homeless by choice, but he stayed homeless by choice to punish himself for perceived mistakes.

What the Goodmans and others miss is that street people don't want to remain homeless for the rest of their lives. Eventually, if they survive, they hit rock bottom and want a change.

What compels a drug addict who has lived in an underground flood channel for several years to make a change? Is it something subtle? Traumatic? Sudden? Gradual? How do they initiate the change? Do they do it on their own or with help?

Half Pint: Two private detectives approached me in the tunnel and said, "Are you Half Pint?"

I said, "Yes, I am."

"Your parents are looking for you."

My parents were watching a special on the tunnels on national TV. I was in the background and they saw me. They freezeframed it and verified it was me, then hired the best of the best to find me. It took the detectives over a month and my parents paid them thirty grand.

That's what it took to finally get me out: the detectives coming down there and me giving them the double-finger and running, and them coming back two days later and throwing a gunny sack over my head and taking me to my parents' hotel room.

Jamie: After almost dying in that fire I went to the Diamond Inn and beat on a door. A hooker I knew was staying there. I went in and took a shower and she GQ'd me out. Gave me clothes and everything. I looked like I walked off the cover of a magazine.

I didn't want anybody to get killed over my bullshit and I wanted to get away from the tunnels and Las Vegas. I knew it was time to go. I called my brother and told him everything and said, "I need to come home."

He sent me 400 bucks and a bus ticket and I left two days later.

David: I was sleeping on a generator box outside the Orleans and this cop came up and said, "You got any warrants?" I had one so they took me to jail for five days.

When I got out I was downtown and I found $100 at the Golden Nugget. I'm planning to get me a girl and some drugs, but I ended up losing the money gambling and got disgusted with myself. Every time a gambler loses his last dollar the first thought that goes through his mind is suicide; instead of doing that I walked to U.S. VETS thinking, I hope they got a bed. If they do I'm going in. I'm through with this shit.

One Shoe Sue: We were making a crack run. Someone had me on his shoulders and I fell and broke my collarbone. He kept going and I ended up crawling, literally, to the Rebel store. That put me in Sunrise Hospital and then a recovery home.

Shortly after that, on Christmas 2011, I told Shaggy, "Let's drink! No one will notice." We brought alcohol into the family house—I'm so ashamed of that—but it was the last drink I had. I don't remember thinking it would be; it wasn't some big revelation. I didn't know I was gonna stop, but I did.

Stephen: I got a good lick one night. Ripped somebody off. Ended up with two big bottles of tequila and a whole bunch of crack rocks.

I'd been in the tunnels three and a half years, and I finally realized no matter how hard I hit that bottle of tequila, no matter how much crack I crammed into that pipe, I couldn't shut it down: the fear, pain, and loneliness I first felt as a teenager on the roof of the International. It was overwhelming.

Shortly after that my nephew, who lived in Tucson and always looked up to me for some reason, said, "We got this veterans hospital here. They got a treatment center. You ready?"

I paused, swallowed, and said, "Yeah, I'm ready."

Eddie: Jodie started getting a disability check and I was working for a temp agency and got a job at a storage yard off Blue Diamond Road. A forklift operator unloading trucks and stacking. I did that in hopes of getting hired permanently.

We bought a scooter so I could get back and forth to work and we saved money and moved into a Siegel Suites motel downtown.

Tex: CrowdRise was the turning point.

I never lost contact with my third wife, Lisa, and she saw the video they put on the Internet to raise money for Shine a Light. She and the man she was living with said they could give me a job. There was only one catch: It started in a week and I had to be in Houston to do it. "Do you want it?" she said.

"Does a frog bump its ass when it hops?"

It was now or never. The opportunity arose and I was ready this time, though part of me wanted to stay. I was comfortable. I was secure. I had that security blanket—the tunnel—as crazy as that may sound.

Ande: One Christmas HELP of Southern Nevada came down with a bunch of undercover cops and dragged us outta the tunnel and the cops said, "If you don't get in the van so these people can help you we're gonna arrest you for trespassing."

ANDE

We get to HELP's office and they don't have housing for us. I started to walk out and they said they could give me a ride. They drove us all the way past Sam Boyd Stadium and threw me out of the van and handed me a bus pass and said, "Merry Christmas!" I hated HELP for that. I would've never reached out to 'em in a million years.

But months later, after I was diagnosed with cancer, they came back down. It was at night and I was sitting on the floor Indian style, listening to music and talking to God. They got on their laptop and typed in the information and were talking to me. They said this is gonna happen and that is gonna happen. I didn't believe a word they said, but two weeks later I was in an apartment.

I left the tunnel because I had breast cancer. I had to stay clean. I was visiting all these doctors and I had to be able to shower, wear proper clothing, and have some decency, because I wasn't a homeless bum. I was a PhD living in a tunnel.

Merch: I met a pretty girl. I liked her and it made me wanna do better in life.

She did heroin and somebody brought her down to the tunnel to see if I could help her get some. Two or three weeks later she came back and I helped her get some more. From there we started hangin' out. She'd stay in the tunnels for a couple days, then leave. We'd spend a weekend together in a motel room, and it was nice being in a comfortable bed and watching TV with a woman I cared about. We started getting a room every weekend and it slowly turned into a relationship.

She's a working girl and she's got some good clients. One got her a two-bedroom apartment and he pays for it six months at a time. He's okay with me staying there. I take care of it, help keep it clean. Her sixteen-year-old son lives there too.

Vegas Dee: After my mom picked me up and we left Las Vegas, we drove to Phoenix. We walked into a trauma center and I was in surgery for eight hours. When I came out I had a huge hole in my neck. When I talked you could see into it. It took a full year for it to close all the way.

The doctor said, "If you do anymore drugs you're going to die. We can get you healthy, but you have to stop using."

Ned: I did an interview a week after Dee left. The reporter came back later and found me and said, "I won $200 at the tables. It's yours and here's a bus ticket. It leaves tonight."

"God bless you, dude! I'll never forget this."

I saved my last bit of heroin for the Greyhound station. I went into the bathroom and shot up.

It was a thirteen-hour trip from Vegas to Denver, and on the way the bus broke down in Vail. The shot had worn off. I started sweating and the guy next to me had a bottle of Jack Daniel's and an ounce of marijuana. The driver said it'd be four to six hours before another bus got there. I was like, You gotta be kidding me. This cat saw me withdrawing and said, "Take a shot of this." Then he said, "Check this out," and he gave me a quarter-bag of weed.

I went outside and smoked and it mellowed me out and I called my mother and said, "I'm hurting. I'm coming in hot. I'm not a pretty sight. If I can get home I hope you will accept me."

My mom said, "Baby, whatever you need. I've never been through what you're going through, but I gotcha."

When I got to my mom's house it was nothing but withdrawals and DTs for a week. I lost control of my urinary system. I shit myself. I soaked the bedsheets with sweat. I stopped cold turkey and my mom took care of me like I was an infant.

I'd kept in contact with Dee and she'd been seeing doctors to find the best way to wean off heroin. She told me about this thing called the "Drug Bomb." It's eleven different supplements three times a day for two weeks. It's supposed to stimulate the neural transmitters and block others that crave the drug. I took it and in a few weeks I was clean.

Jazz: A few friends babysat me as best as they could when I was dealing with the loss of Sharon. I was on a mission to stay as fucked up as possible or to overdose if God would let me. I couldn't drink enough or do enough meth.

I moved back to the spot after Sharon passed. I don't know why. Trying to rebuild, I guess. That was our home. That's where I felt closest to her. Maybe being down there was a way for me to find closure.

I don't know why it took something so devastating to finally make me wanna change. I always wanted to get outta there with her. I went to Veterans Village, but it just seemed pointless. One night I was sitting in my room and the only thing that stopped me from committing suicide was I couldn't get the rope through the ceiling vent. I made a noose, but couldn't find anywhere to hang it.

Someone knocked on the door. It was my ride to the bus station. I left everything in the room and tunnel and got on a bus to Arizona to stay with Yvette, a long-lost love who'd come back into my life. She contacted me after seeing a GoFundMe page I put up to raise money for Sharon's funeral.

After I lost Sharon, I was staying at the Motel 6 on Trop and Koval, and I made contact with my daughter Danielle and grandson Sky. The last time I'd seen my daughter she was five. But after I got in touch she came and visited me at the motel. I was so busted up from the flood I couldn't walk. It took me ten minutes to walk ten feet to the bathroom. Her and I talked for over an hour and we kept in touch when I was in Arizona.

I was supposed to stay in Arizona only for Christmas, but it got extended till the end of February. I got clean and sober and took a hard look at myself. Did a lotta thinking, a lotta crying.

Yvette and her mom and their dogs got me through some emotional times. I was lost. Plus I had prison time hanging over my head for a warrant. We all knew I had to turn myself in to clear that up, so I did at the end of February.

Misty: I found out I was pregnant. I was staying in the tunnels, a park, Siegel Suites, Shelter Island, wherever I could. One day, dead tired in the park, I handed my pipe to a kid, gave away the drugs I had, gave away my cigarettes. I got up and looked at everybody.

"Fuck you! Fuck the tunnels! Fuck this park! Fuck alcohol! Fuck drugs!" Then I called U.S. VETS and said, "Can somebody pick me up? I'm ready."

I checked into the hospital on July 1. My water broke the morning of July 4. I had my kid at 10:13 the night of the Fourth. I got off the streets and gained my independence, then lost it again on Independence Day.

Seven pounds, fifteen ounces. A healthy baby boy. I realized then that my life was worth keeping. I said, "I'm gonna name him Keeper." I gave him his father's middle name. Keeper Lee.

TK: My dog Spanger hurt himself trying to hop over a wall. That sucked, especially since we didn't have much money at the time. Luckily the Sandy Hill Animal Clinic helped us out.

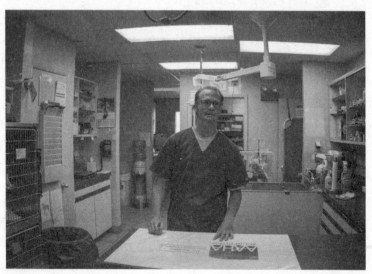

TK

Spanger could barely walk because of the injury and he was getting older. Every time we left the tunnel we'd have to lift him over the wall. Eventually we ended up staying in the desert, but he started having trouble with his shoulder. Then he lost use of his legs. He was in pain and we had to do what was best for him, so the vet put him down. When they put him down I put the pipe down.

It was tough knowing I couldn't do anything for Spanger, so I did what I could do: I changed my life.

When Spanger passed away I wanted to do better, but I had no job history. I figured the only way to solve that problem was to get an education, so I went to the College of Southern Nevada. Eventually I got a job at the Sandy Hill Animal Clinic. They knew I hadn't worked, but they saw me taking steps to be a better person, so they worked with me.

I'm a kennel technician and vet assistant. I do a lot of cleaning because I know how to do that and it gives everybody else more time to do what they know. When I'm done with that I help with the procedures. I read the log and help administer drugs to the animals. I walk 'em. I hold 'em so other people can assist them.

I'm always there a half hour early. I'm responsible. I'm a hard worker. I still need more education though, which is why I'm going to Pima Medical school.

Shaggy: Two cops and a cricket saved my life.

I was sitting on my bed, wearing a headlamp, and had my stuff spread out on my lap and was preparing to shoot up, and this big, black cricket bounced into my line of sight. I looked at it and said, "Don't do it!"

Sure enough, it flew up at me and I dropped everything.

I tried to catch that cricket for hours. At the end of that time I found a bright flashlight. Two cops. I told 'em my

SHAGGY

name and Social and, because I had a warrant, they asked how long it would take me to get my stuff together.

I said, "A few minutes."

"All right. Meet us outside."

I woke up my girlfriend and grabbed my stuff and we ran out the other end of the tunnel. All I needed was a cigarette and soda. I got 'em, then waited for the cops in the parking lot.

I got a public defender I'd had before. I'd asked him to help me get jail time on the weekends, which you can do in certain situations, and he did, but I blew it off. The first thing he said to me this time around was, "You couldn't make the weekends, huh?" Then he said, "How about trying the drug-court program?"

I ended up doing really well in the program. I got MVP and a job at the carwash next to the tunnel entrance. I worked there from four months of sobriety to twenty-two months. I saw the people I'd lived with and did what I could to help them with encouraging words and a few dollars here or there. I ended up being a supervisor at the carwash, and they all watched me grow outta that stage of my life.

Knyck: The cops were coming down and asking questions. "Is there a runaway here?" The people Maddie and I were living with didn't like that and they kicked her out, but I wasn't gonna let her hit the streets by herself. I was invested in her. We were together at that point.

We moved to the Trop and Eastern area, and it all ended one day. I got hemmed up by her dad and he called the cops. It was her sixteenth birthday. They put me in handcuffs and threw me into the back seat. I mouthed through the window, "Happy birthday. I love you."

I ended up doing eighteen months for statutory rape. Me going to prison was the best thing that could've happened to us. It probably saved our lives.

I thought it was better not to get involved with Maddie again, but I wanted to check in with her. We'd been apart two years while I was in jail and prison. I hadn't seen or heard from her at all. Had no idea if she was alive.

I was staying at Catholic Charities 'cause I just got outta prison, and I sent her a message on Facebook: "I'm sorry and I hope I didn't do anything to hurt you. Here's my number if you wanna talk." I was just trying to say I wish I could've been a better influence. I'd been rehabilitated to believe I'd done something horrible.

She called immediately and said, "You wanna meet at Starbucks?"

I said yeah, and we've been together ever since.

Easy E: I stole $100 from Phil. I'd stolen from people before, including the old lady at the Gold Coast, but Phil was my best friend, the person who looked out for me day after day, the one who would've put a knife to somebody's throat if they messed with me.

On December 31 me and Phil talked things through. He said, "I got a dude who wants us to help him move and he's going to give us each a hundred bucks." That's how I paid him back. Then he went and got a dime bag and rolled a couple joints and he got me a bag of dope too. I shot dope five minutes to midnight on New Year's Eve. Right as the clock was about to strike midnight I fired up a joint. I exhaled and walked along the railroad tracks, so I could watch the fireworks over the Strip geeked out and stoned.

The next day that HELP was open I walked into their office. I was sitting in the lobby and Phil walked in. I said, "What are you doing here?"

"The same thing you are. We got in this together; we're gonna get out of it together too."

Rich Penksa had said any day you come to the office I'll put you in housing. He walked in the lobby, shook his head, and said, "I never thought I'd see the day. You two, into my office."

We were in a van thirty minutes later. Rich took us back to our camps to see if we had anything left, because it had rained, and the only thing there was Phil's stash.

I said, "Dude, don't you fucking dare!" He fired it up.

As we were walking back to meet Rich, Phil said, "Are my eyes buggin'?"

"Put on your sunglasses, man!"

Rich took us to a halfway house in the south part of town. It was a $650,000 home. It had a pool, barbecue grill. A really nice place, though the manager never paid his power bill.

Phil: There were times I thought about getting out of the tunnels. If someone gave me that chance I was gonna ride it all the way outta there. That's all I needed—a stepping stone.

The last hurrah was five minutes before I got into Rich's van. Me and Easy went to the spot, and my stash was there and I smoked it, and that was it. I haven't touched it since.

I was messaging with Easy one night at my apartment and was also on a poker site. There was a girl on the site who was wearing a Yankees jersey in her profile picture. I'm a Red Sox fan so you know I'm gonna talk some shit. I told her I didn't like the jersey, but I like what's in it, and we ended up messaging for over an hour.

We exchanged numbers and talked three or four times a day. She turned out to be my angel. She'd listen to me vent. She'd encourage me. One day she said, "You wanna get away from Vegas and leave everything behind?"

I moved to Odessa, Texas, on April 1, 2013. That was a sad day for me because it was my granddaughter's first birthday and I couldn't be there, but we celebrated it the weekend before I left Las Vegas. On her first birthday I was getting on a plane to start a new life.

Tommy: I met Big Tim from HELP when I was panhandling on the Strip. He said he could help me.

I said, "What are you gonna do? Buy me a case of beer?"

"I'll help you get off the street."

TOMMY

"Get lost, dude."

He handed me his card and said, "When you're ready gimme a call. We'll get you an apartment, job, everything."

I went to his office the next Monday. I wasn't drunk, but I had alcohol on my breath and he had asked me not to drink. I told him I couldn't sign the papers unless I had a few drinks because I couldn't stop shaking. I signed the papers and said, "Okay. Let's go look at my apartment."

"It's not that simple," he said. "First I gotta take you to WestCare."

That's why I'll never drink or do drugs again. While at WestCare I went into shock. I started flopping around, going through withdrawals from the alcohol. They had to zap me back to life.

I ended up getting sober and I called Tim and said, "Come and get me and let's go see my apartment."

"I'll pick you up, but we can't go to an apartment. I gotta take you to a sober-living home."

That's where I met Phil and Easy E.

Phil got outta the sober-living home and I went to visit him. He was living in an apartment near the Boulevard Mall. I said I wanna see if I can live there too.

Tim said, "You can move in there, but you're gonna have to wait another few weeks 'cause the apartment's empty."

He showed me the apartment and I said, "You don't have *any* furniture?"

"All I got is some lawn furniture."

"That'll do."

"What?"

"Two lawn chairs and a patio table will be fine."

"You gotta have a bed."

He took me to Walmart and bought me a blow-up mattress and I said, "Now can I move into my apartment?"

He smiled and said, "Yeah."

Skip: After the doctors saved my arm and I rehabbed it I went to Catholic Charities. Best move I could've made. I was living there and was head steward in the dining hall. They couldn't believe the way I was working. I was stocking water and three different refrigerators, cleaning, taking out the trash, but it ended up being a little too much for my arm.

I met this guy Vinnie through Catholic Charities and he says, "I got a job for you. It's for a celebrity."

Next thing I know I'm working for music producer Teddy Riley, helping him build a studio in Las Vegas. Being a musician, it was a dream job. I did that for six months and found out more about who he is and what he wrote. We became friends. He's done a lot for me. He got me back interested in music. I'm starting to drum again. My arm feels fine.

Barry: I became friends with a neighbor of mine when I was in HELP's program. Later we got offered a bus ticket outta town and he had family in Jacksonville, Florida, so we came here and I was able to find work at a tree-service company, one of the largest in the area and growing. Got my commercial driver's license so I can drive the trucks. I'm part of the ground crew and in a couple weeks I'll be a foreman.

I'm living about a mile from the office in a two-bedroom house. Got my own bathroom, kitchen. Don't have to share it with anyone except two cats.

Most of my co-workers know about my prison time and time in the tunnels. I showed 'em a video on YouTube and they responded well to my story. They've gotten to know me. They don't judge me for my past. They judge me for who I am today.

Becky: I'd given Zero a million ultimatums and we finally hustled up enough money to get a weekly that we didn't lose after seven days. Then I got my daughter back. Me and Zero were still using and were about to lose our room, and I looked around and saw my kid and I just couldn't do it to her or myself anymore. I knew Zero's mom had wanted him to come home for a long time, and he called her and she said we could all come there. I'll never forget that moment.

I've moved around and started over and gotten sober a thousand times, but it never felt as good as it did this time. Zero's mom and her husband Roger had worked their whole lives and had this beautiful land and home in Philadelphia, Mississippi, and they were willing to buy us new clothes and food and everything. It was an easy transition.

The agreement when we moved there was that one of us had to work, and Zero wanted to do that. He got a job at a hospital and I stayed home and took care of the dogs and cleaned the house and cooked dinner.

I was overjoyed when I found out I was pregnant. Zero had been telling me he was sterile. I looked at the pregnancy as the universe giving us a gift for being clean.

Zero: I knew Becky was pregnant two days before she said anything. She was acting weird. She came in the house, walked right past me with her purse under her arm, and went into the bathroom and shut the door.

When she told me she was pregnant it was the happiest day of my life. I thought I couldn't have kids. But she didn't know how I'd respond.

"Do you wanna talk about an abortion?" she said.

"Are you outta your mind?" I was so excited. I knew it was gonna be a boy.

Szmauz: I equate it to a God intervention. It was like someone dragged me out of the tunnel into the light and said, "Look at yourself! What are you doing?"

I was covered head to toe in soot. The light was blinding. I could barely move.

I called my mom, bawling my eyes out, and she asked if I was really gonna do it this time.

She'd been trying to find a place that could help me and she told me about Origins Recovery Center. I left Las Vegas at midnight on a Greyhound bound for south Texas.

It was a nighttime meeting at Origins and I was talking about being in Vegas and living in the tunnels. I was saying how no one could relate to my story because it was so crazy—I'm from New Hampshire, I'm a musician, the border crossings into Mexico, the Las Vegas tunnels—and someone behind me said, "I was in the Vegas tunnels too."

I looked back and there's this dude dressed like a pirate. I thought, Who the hell is this guy? He seemed wicked cool.

Turns out it was Rick. He and Cyndi were at Origins too and he was working on this pirate-themed cruise and he came to the meeting right after work. I considered myself a gypsy pirate. My family's from Poland and they were gypsies. We started talking after the meeting and he was a really big help to me. It made me feel less secluded in what I was going through. It helped me realize I wasn't fighting this battle alone.

Rick: I was depressed and somebody told me a story about a couple in another tunnel. The guy OD'd and left his wife alone. HELP got her out and into an apartment. I thought, Maybe they could do that for Cyndi? I was hiding a gun in the tunnel for somebody and the thought crossed my mind to use it on myself.

That night I said a prayer and cried myself to sleep. I'd been up for four days, only two of them on drugs. The rest of it was stress.

About an hour after I went to sleep a light shined in my face. It was the cops. As they were searching the tunnel I told them I had two felony warrants and was going to be leaving with them tonight. They said they appreciated my honesty.

When I got released, Cyndi was outside the jail waiting for me.

"I'm with our ride," she said.

"Ride? What's going on?"

"It's a surprise, but a good one. It's gonna be awkward, but I think you're gonna like it."

We get into this really nice car. There are two women in it who are dressed up. One of 'em turns to me and says, "You must be Rick. I'm a producer with the *Dr. Phil* show."

Dr. Phil filmed us in the tunnel and filmed Cyndi and her daughters in studio. For the studio shoot they put us in a hotel in some shitty L.A. neighborhood. I went outside for a walk, being my usual tweaker self, just seeing what was around. There was a cameraman hiding in a bush. I'm sure they expected us to go out looking for drugs or to the liquor store.

I remember getting ready to go on stage. Cyndi was crying and scared and she said, "I can't believe we're gonna be on the *Dr. Phil* show."

I turned to her and said, "At least it's not *Jerry Springer.*"

At the end of the shoot they explained that they were getting me and Cyndi a place to live for a year. They said we wouldn't have any responsibilities.

We talked about it and came to the conclusion that we'd fuck up everything they did for us. We were drug addicts and needed help for our addictions. They said, Funny you should mention that. There's this treatment center called Origins that we're thinking about sending you to.

Me and Cyndi both said, "You need to do that before you do anything else for us."

Szmauz was telling everyone they didn't understand him. He was too far gone. Rehab wasn't gonna work for him. "I'm gonna do my time, then go back out and take the biggest shot I can and kill myself. That's the only life I know."

I spoke up and shared my story: "I have a job. I make twenty-five dollars an hour and can work three hours a day or six. I make people laugh. I get to fire cannons. I'm having a blast, pun intended. I'm clean. I share an apartment with the woman I love. I don't deserve any of this. I'm a junkie from the tunnels of Vegas. I had to crawl up fifteen feet just to get my mind in the gutter."

His eyes lit up. He actually started crying.

I got to talk to him after the meeting and he said, "You were in the Vegas tunnels?"

I said yeah and told him where.

He said he knew the tunnel because he'd stayed in one not far from there. Then he asked how long I'd been sober.

"Two years."

"So this can work for me?"

"Absolutely!"

Now he's coming up on two years of sobriety himself.

ROADBLOCKS

The route from the storm drains of Las Vegas to serenity aboveground is anything but direct. It's circuitous, potholed, composed of dangerous curves and hairpin turns, and susceptible to roadblocks and detours. To those navigating the course, it can be compared to driving over the Himalayas without brakes.

One question informs this chapter: What was the most difficult part of transitioning out of the tunnels? The responses range from PTSD to finding work, learning to use new technologies, or simply staying sober.

To extend the road-trip analogy, most of the interviewees made a few wrong turns. Who corrected, learned from their mistakes, and stayed the course? Who fell by the wayside or made a U-turn, ending up back where they started?

One Shoe Sue: Learning how to take a shower and find a job. Looking people in the eye, especially my mom and dad. All the shameful things I did to my family and kids. That was the hardest thing—coming clean. Just showing my face to my mom and dad and sons was one of the hardest things I've done in my life.

Ande: Because I got outta the tunnel and into an apartment I was getting chemo once a month. That was bad enough, but it was also causing sciatica and I couldn't walk. I was in agony. I had to quit one of the two jobs I had. It was that painful.

Melinda: I have a brain injury from when Manny threw me against the wall. I have dementia. I get lost. I get panic attacks.

Tommy: I was a mean person when I was getting sober. I wasn't used to my new personality. You have to take on a whole different persona and I was used to being a happy drunk. It took six months for me to be halfway nice.

One of the other clients at HELP said something to me at the apartments by the mall. I grabbed him and had him hanging over the balcony railing. His caseworker came to me later and said, "You can't be doing that, Tommy!"

I said, "Shut the fuck up or you're gonna be hanging there too!"

Barry: HELP's job-readiness workshop. At the workshop we had to do mock interviews. I'm not someone that likes talking to people, so having to do that was hard. Dressing up in a suit. When you're not comfortable in a suit it shows.

TK: Not having that instant gratification. On the street everything happens so fast. You need to make money? You just walk to the corner and ask someone for it.

Things are slower, but I respect the money I make. I make less at the animal clinic than I did panhandling, but I save more.

Rick: One thing that messed me up was my biggest character defect, which I found out more about at Origins. I was reminded that I was a bad provider for myself and Cyndi: financially, emotionally, physically, in every way. I'd get jobs and work them for a couple months, then find something wrong with them and quit. I played the victim.

In recovery I fell back into that pattern. Working several jobs and not doing the stuff I'd promised to do, and my old way of thinking started to creep back in. I wasn't going to meetings, I wasn't sponsoring any guys, I wasn't meeting with my sponsors. I wasn't happy with anything and I was thinking about using again.

The hardest thing for me was accepting that I was doing things my way again and seeing that it was gonna take me back to where I was before.

Misty: I'd been friends with this guy for years, but we hadn't seen each other in a while. Ended up running into him at college a few years after I had Keeper. He was going for massage therapy and I was going for phlebotomy and medical assisting.

We ended up getting together. Lo and behold, after one little go 'round, I was pregnant again. Good times.

He put a ring on my finger, made all these promises, then he went to work one day and didn't come home. This girl posted on Facebook that she's at a bar having adult beverages with him and a few other people.

I called him and said, "What's going on?"

Turns out he'd been seeing her this whole time. He said, "It is what it is. I don't have to explain myself to anybody. I'm in love with her. It's her I need to be with and nobody else."

Shaggy: I'd get anxiety when it rained. I didn't realize what was going on at first, but then it clicked: That's the way it was down there. When you saw rain clouds you got really nervous.

Working at the carwash by the tunnel and seeing the guys and knowing I couldn't be a part of that anymore. All I could be was a friend, somebody that could relate, but couldn't really help them or support what they were doing. They'd ask to use my phone and I couldn't let 'em because I knew who they were calling. I had to draw boundaries.

Tex: I'll be walking down the street and I'll think people are looking at me like I'm a homeless piece of shit. I got a place to live. I got a job. I'm clean-shaven, don't stink, I wear nice clothes. I look like a regular member of society, but there's still part of me that thinks people are staring and laughing at me or making fun of me.

The hardest thing is getting that outta my head. Hey, I am somebody. I'm a beneficial member of society.

Having to be around people. I'm reclusive. Mamma always told me, "People are gonna get you in trouble, boy!" So I started distancing myself from them, and being homeless and in the tunnels only distances you further.

I'm working at a wedding venue now outside of Houston and I'm around a lotta people, and I have to handle them differently than I did when I was homeless. The people I was around when I was homeless were usually fucking with me and I had to have a certain mentality. I had to be hard, stone cold. I said whatever I thought. Now I have to watch what I say and how I say it.

That's been hard: putting my brain in gear before my mouth starts moving.

Half Pint: I have trouble sleeping when it's quiet, when I don't have to have one eye open. I still can't sleep with my bedroom door closed. I rent a room in a house near Trop and Fort Apache, and I never close my bedroom door. It's too confined. I don't know if it's from the tunnels or it's just me. I have PTSD from my nails being pulled off, being raped, and just surviving down there.

I go to this twelve-step meeting every Wednesday night and one of the protocols is that everyone introduces themselves. All of a sudden I heard a voice from the past and got really scared. I immediately recognized the voice as somebody who had done bad things to me in the tunnels.

A decade later, when this person appeared at the meeting, my head immediately went back to the tunnels and the fear I lived with down there, and I didn't know what to do. I knew I was safe. I knew I was with people who loved and cared for me. But this was none of their business. It wasn't their problem.

The guy approached me after the meeting wanting to apologize. I told him I hoped he got sober, I hoped he stayed sober, I hoped he found what I found through these meetings, but please stay away from me.

Later I spoke to my sponsor and that changed my perspective. I thought, Someone gave me a chance to get sober. They overlooked bad things I'd done in the past. Who am I to judge whether somebody has the right to sobriety?

In recovery we all have to own up to what we've done in the past. We have to make amends. But there's a time and place for that.

Stephen: I was sober for a year and things were good. I was in touch with my family. I had a job at the Hilton in Tucson. I had a car, an apartment. Then I got too busy to do what I'd been doing—reading the Big Book, going to meetings, praying—and I got drunk and ended up where I always do: curled in a ball, crying.

I called my brother, who was also in recovery. "Dave, how you doing?"

"Great. You?"

"Not so good."

"Call your sponsor."

"I could hardly call you."

"Go to a meeting."

"I'm afraid to open the door." I threw down the phone and curled tighter on the floor, like I'd done so many times in the tunnels.

A short time later there was a knock at the door. I'll never forget that sound. I got up and wiped my eyes and looked through the peephole. It was my brother. He flew 400 miles to see if I was okay.

When I opened the door I had a moment of clarity. We went to a meeting and I finally heard what my sponsor had told me a year earlier: If I read the Book, go to meetings, and pray, I don't have to die in the tunnels under Paradise.

I've been doing that ever since, some days better than others.

Zero: Things were good. I left the hospital job and was working at the casino at the Choctaw reservation and loving being a father. Then my sister killed herself and that messed me up real bad. I was pretty messed up already because my old hustling partner Bobby had killed himself before that.

I was depressed and Becky felt like she couldn't help or comfort me. I put up a wall between us and we grew further and further apart.

I'm still mad and sad. It pisses me off. I love Becky. I never cheated on her. I told her if she was gonna cheat just break up with me, but she did it anyway and hid it from me and kept doing it. That's wrong, man!

You shouldn't take other people's iPads with you when you're sneaking around. It pings locations. She kept taking my iPad, then I saw this address and went there because she didn't pick me up from work and wouldn't answer her phone. There's our truck sitting in front of this house. I knocked on the door. Some guy answered and said she wasn't there. He told me to leave or he'd call the police.

My mom wouldn't let me throw Becky outta the house. I had her shit and was dragging it out, but Mom stopped me. I wound up having to leave for a while. Kicked outta my own house.

Becky: Zero started doing Adderall, then I did too and we relapsed. I was unfaithful to him and we broke up, but we're both sober now and we talk every day and we still love each other very much.

Iron: I'm just trying to stay outta jail, stay sober, and stay in touch with my family. I'm falling out with them again. They don't approve of me not having a steady job. They think I should be doing other things than what I'm doing, and they may be right.

My relationship with my daughter is about the same as it was after *The Buried Life* show. Well, it's probably deteriorated a little. She's not mad at me or anything, but she's not happy with me either.

I got tired of Vegas and came back to Oklahoma and got a job washing and painting oil-field equipment and was makin' good money. One day I ended up with too much time on my hands and too much money in my pocket. I got ahold of some people, and next thing you know I was back on the dope.

I'm not sober, but I'm not nearly as fucked up as I was in the tunnels. I have my clean days.

I do the least amount of wrong I can. That's the simplest way to put it.

Manny: Honestly, for me and Melinda, the hardest part was gaining weight. I went from 225 pounds to 315 and Melinda gained weight too. That was probably the worst part: seeing how sad it made her to be fat.

"Get that pig outta the way!" We were crossing Maryland Parkway and she could hardly move and someone yelled that at her from a car. It was fucked up. Her brother had just died. OD'd. And she was really missing her children.

All that took a toll on her.

I was in HELP's program till September of last year, then I used again. I was high all the time. Me and Melinda broke up. I got what I deserved. I'm back on the street, but I'm fighting the good fight. Eighteen days sober.

I'm trying not to do crystal because of the voices. The shit I hear. Scary shit. Plus it fucked up my relationship, my job, and everything else. I didn't care about anything except that dark-ass crystal meth.

Pretty Boy Steve: HELP made it so easy, so comfortable, so fast that I guess me and Kat took it for granted. Before you knew it we were back in the tunnels.

When you're housed and you go by the tunnels you say, "I ain't never going back there. I don't care what happens." And then everything you said you wouldn't do you end up doing.

Kat was crying. She didn't wanna go back down there. We fought it hard, but your body gives up. Your brain gets tired. You gotta sleep for crying out loud. I can't sleep at a bus stop with people all around me or in a sportsbook, so there we were with two thin bed sheets and it was cold

KAT

and all we were thinking about was where we could put our heads down without being bothered, and that was the tunnels.

The first two or three nights back we cried ourselves to sleep. We couldn't believe we were down there again.

Phil: Everybody slipped. There were occasions that presented themselves. I'm not gonna sit here and say I didn't slip, but I never let it take me back down.

My kids kept me on track. I was in contact with my oldest, and my youngest lived in Vegas and she knew I'd been on the streets doing bad things for years. When I got into the program and got my head outta my ass, she came to see me and realized the transformation I went through. That was my driving force to stay on track.

Easy E: Me and Phil walked into HELP's office with literally the clothes on our back. They got us our food-stamp card and dropped us off at the halfway house. It was nice being able to take a shit whenever you wanted without having to press your ass against a concrete wall and wiping with a dirty sock. Being able to shower. When I was homeless I once went eight months without a shower, without a single drop of water hitting my body.

Those new things were amazing, but I had to learn or relearn everything. I remember my first luffa sponge. It was in the bathroom at the halfway house and I go, "What the fuck is this?"

One of the guys tells me how to use it and I'm like, He's nuts. I go into the shower with a bar of soap and give it a try and it lathered right up. I was amazed.

I couldn't remember how to use a grill. I'm sticking the lighter underneath it and this guy goes, "Just hit the button, buddy." The button? What?

I saw Wes, who was once my best friend on the streets, coming out of Harrah's one day and he looked right past me. He weighed about a buck twenty. I could see every bone in his face. I turned my head and walked away and went down the escalator bawling my eyes out. I couldn't even say hello to someone who used to be a dear friend. I knew if I spent any time with him I'd be back on the dope.

One day a friend of mine said, "I'm going to an NA meeting."

I said, "I wanna go." I was done with counseling and was going crazy. I wanted to get high.

I walked into the meeting and they were giving out clean tags and the guy running it said, "Anyone got twenty-four hours clean?"

I went up and got my tag. "My name's Eric and I'm an addict."

"Anyone got thirty days clean?" I went up again.

"Sixty days?"

Every time he called out days I went up and got my tag and said it again: "My name's Eric and I'm an addict."

Finally he said to me, "How many more of these you gonna get? You got two years?"

"No, but I will in a few weeks."

Everybody laughed, and that's when I realized how far I'd come.

ROAD TO REDEMPTION PART II

Melinda: Praying I'd get ahold of my kids—that's what I was doing every day in the tunnels and when Manny and I got an apartment. My kids were my first thought when I woke and my last thought before I went to sleep. I knew I couldn't get custody of them. All I could do was look for them online and wait till they got old enough that they could contact me.

Two years ago, on Mother's Day, my daughter Alycia called and said, "Mom, we all wanna see you."

I went to her house and was so nervous, and my little boy Anthony, who's now a young man, was the first to come to the door and he gave me a big hug. My daughters Vanessa and Christianni were there too.

I kept in touch with them after that and started moving toward them and away from relationships and drinking and the streets. I didn't wanna put anything above them like I did before. Now I'm living with two of them, and Christianni visits, and I just reunited with my first born, Alex.

"Mom." I love hearing that word. I thank God when I'm cooking them dinner or washing their clothes. I love doing the little "mom" things.

Maddie: Knyck and I are living in an apartment near Las Vegas Boulevard and Serene. I'm going to cosmetology school to get my license to do hair, which is a dream of mine,

KNYCK AND MADDIE

and he's working for the Democratic National Committee making phone calls.

I need 1,600 hours to get my cosmetology license and I have 996. I've reconnected with my family and have been spending a lot of time with them and they've accepted Knyck. He's moved up so far in their eyes that he actually goes to Thanksgiving and Christmas dinner. Going from where they sent him to prison to having holiday dinners together—that's crazy. They can see he cares. On the streets he'd fly a sign for seven or eight hours before he let me work. A lotta guys wouldn't do that. They'd send the female out because she'd make more money.

We've been sober for a couple years and plan on getting married once we've saved enough cash.

Szmauz: Since graduating from Origins and moving back to New Hampshire I met the love of my life, who's also a musician. Her name's Gwen. She's amazing.

The drummer in my current band plays a lotta open-mic nights. I'd just released a CD so I went to this open mic with him and was selling it there. She was sitting at the bar waiting for her turn to play.

I was like, "Yo! Buy my CD!"

She said, "I'd like to, but I don't have any money." I gave her one for free.

As the drummer and I were leaving to go to another open mic I turned to her and said, "Come to J's or you're a nerd!"

She showed up and we've been inseparable ever since.

Ned: I'm working for the number one car dealership in Colorado. A Nissan store. I average twenty to twenty-five sells and make $8,000 to $12,000 a month.

I'm engaged. I proposed to my new lady in December. She's a stellar mom. She deserves it, I deserve it, her baby girl deserves it. Her daughter turns six today. We're preparing for her birthday party.

My lady rented and decorated a little venue, and my mom's grocery store is catering the party. She opened an ethnic store that imports stuff from Poland: meats, produce, pickles.

I'm the happiest man on Earth.

Vegas Dee: I've been clean three years and I'm living in Florida with my mom. I didn't realize how bad I needed some Southern hospitality. It's been nice. I work for an animal hospital under five phenomenal doctors. My title is receptionist, but I also get to work in the operating room and kennel. I've learned and grown so much. I feel more alive and back to myself than I have in a long time.

I've also realized I'm a nice person. I can be, even when someone is like, "You need to hand me that pen!"

The street side of me wants to say, "Bitch, pick up the pen yourself and sign the damn paper!" But I hold it in and say, "Yes, ma'am. I'm happy to help you with that."

No one here knows about my old life: the website in Atlanta, the drugs, the tunnels, all the hustling I did with Ned. They have no idea. I keep it tucked away and hidden behind a smile.

I made amends with my dad. I forgave him. I just let it go. I didn't want the affliction to be on me anymore, and I'd caused enough pain to other people that I had to own my shit and forgive other people for theirs.

The last time I spoke to Ned was over the holidays. He told me he was engaged and I congratulated him and wished him the best.

I said, "I can finally let you go."

He said, "Yeah, you can."

Jamie: I came back to Mississippi on the bus and went straight into the studio. A longtime friend who owns the studio honored his commitment. He'd said, "Dude, come here and stay and do some session work. I can always use a guitarist."

I'm livin' in the studio in downtown Leland. It's Main Street now, but it's the old Highway 61. Right across the street is a bar called Ruby's that's falling apart, but Muddy Waters played there, B.B. King, Son House, all those cats.

It's inspiring. This morning I started writing a song because a buddy of mine is getting married. I've always had this idea that people are meant to find their soulmate, the person they really connect with. Not many people find that, but my friend Tim is getting married to his soulmate Michelle, and I'm writing a song for the occasion.

My song "Comes a Storm" is based on my time in the tunnels. Me, Kregg, Jazz, and Zero were sitting on a mattress smoking meth and laughing about the fact that water was flowing past us. It was almost time to go. We had our shit stowed and a room at the Diamond Inn. There was a clap of thunder and somebody, I don't remember who, said, "Comes a storm, gentlemen."

When I heard that the guitar riff immediately played in my head—the A minor picking part that goes dramatically down through several keys and comes back up. It stuck in my head. When I got to the studio I laid down that track first. It's an instrumental.

Rick: I started getting out there and helping guys in recovery, and I found comfort in it. That led to me working at Origins as a recovery advocate, showing other guys how I got clean. I love my job. I've never had a job where I got called in on my day off and was excited about it. This job does that for me.

I can wake in the morning and be discouraged from the day before, and what motivates me and gets me out of bed is helping these guys. I get to share what I've learned and how I learned it. It's an awesome thing, man. Sometimes it doesn't seem real. Other times, when I look back on my life in the tunnels, that doesn't seem real.

Cyndi: Me and Rick have a good relationship with my kids. We get to visit 'em twice a year for a couple weeks each time.

While we were in treatment my youngest daughter and my son came to the family week program, where they teach families about everything we learn at Origins and they get to say what's on their mind. All the things my daughter couldn't say on *Dr. Phil* she said to my face in a safe environment, and that's the moment we started bonding. A few months later I was in her wedding. I never thought that would be possible.

Last year my daughter Amber was pregnant and she invited me to be her birthing partner, which was an amazing experience. The bond we created through that was incredible. To hold that little baby in my arms.

One Shoe Sue: I worked at Taco Bell and Dairy Queen, but I quit Taco Bell when I became more permanent with DQ. I've been working at DQ for five years. I'm general manager.

It's a fun little store. We do cakes, ice cream, and novelties. I don't do much physical work myself because I'm the manager and I've learned to delegate with some confidence. I came into the job kinda nervous because I didn't understand any of the computer stuff.

My boss said, "Where've you been? Living under a rock?"

I wasn't welcomed at the family home for many years. Now I'm living there. I went to court last year to get custody of

ONE SHOE SUE

my younger son. I needed to provide a home for him, and my father offered to let us live there.

My older son, Shaggy, was mad at me for years. We didn't really know each other. But I love him and am so proud of him. I wish I could take credit for the man he's become.

There's a process in the twelve-step program where you make amends. I went to him and we decided it'd be best if we let bygones be bygones, because there's a lot of bitter, longstanding feelings between us.

My children were my guilt trip for a long time, but I'm not alone in that. A lotta people share that same story.

I was volunteering at a women's recovery center and the housemother said, "Sue, we need to help this girl!" She was outside in a car with her boyfriend. She had no bra on, she was wearing boy shorts, her arm was broken. He was pushing her outta the car saying, "I'll kill her if you don't take her!"

We took her in and gave her a bed. She started to get sober and I got to know her. I was her sponsor.

Shaggy saw her at a meeting and said, "Who's that?"

"Kaylyn," I said.

She was still at the stage where she had to focus on herself, so we couldn't introduce 'em for a while. But when they did meet it took off.

Shaggy: After I graduated from the drug-court program, Freedom House opened a new inpatient treatment center and I ended up being the lead case manager there. We work with clients who come straight outta jail with prison sentences hanging over their heads. This is their last chance to get on their feet. We help them get IDs, birth certificates, and Social Security cards. We get them enrolled in school if they need a GED as part of their parole conditions. We get 'em food stamps. We help 'em transition back into the real world.

I also communicate with the drug courts and write reviews on 'em. I went from being a client in that system—I can find my name in every program I use—to case-managing clients in it.

I don't know much about my mom's tunnel story. We spoke about it briefly, but she lived in a different tunnel at a different time. It wasn't till I was sober for a year or so that I realized she'd lived down there too. That's part of how we rekindled our relationship, having that connection.

Our relationship is strong today, but I had to learn a lot about her and she had to learn a lot about me too.

I first saw Kaylyn at a twelve-step meeting and I remember looking over at my friend and mouthing across the room, "I'm in love!"

The rule at the treatment center is guys and girls are not allowed to talk to each other, so I patiently waited for her treatment to end. I intended to introduce myself as soon as possible.

The day she got outta treatment she friended me on Facebook and we texted the entire night. For the next six months we got to spend one day a week together, and for the first time in both of our lives we built a solid foundation for a relationship.

We were at the courthouse one day and we walked past the marriage bureau. Since we'd played around with the idea of getting married, Kaylyn suggested we see how much it'd cost to get a license. When we got to the window and were told the price she asked me if I had the cash. I had no doubt she was who I wanted to spend the rest of my life with, so I paid for the license, no questions asked, and six months later we were married. We'd agreed that we should wait for her to be clean one year before we made any big life changes; we were married the day after her one-year anniversary of being clean.

Now we have a son, a house. I've been clean two and a half years. My mom and family are back in my life. I love my job.

If you had told me that in two and half years my life could be so different I would've made the change sooner. But I don't think you could've convinced me things could ever be this good.

HALF PINT

Half Pint: I got my teaching license back. It's on my fridge. I'm proud of it. Then this Middle Eastern family found me. They're royalty and they have a handicapped child: autism, cerebral palsy, a speech impediment. They asked me to do a demo lesson for 'em. I was five years sober at the time and they hired me as his homeschool teacher. I work at their estate and go through the security gates. I've been with 'em three years.

I'm drivin' my dad's old PT Cruiser. He said when I got two years sober I could have it. I also finally got the key to the storage unit where they put all my stuff when I left Montevista.

This is my seventeenth rehab and I've been sober for eight years, three months, and fifteen days, not that anyone's counting. I didn't have any options this time. They found me in the tunnels. Where can you go from there?

Stephen: Around year two of sobriety I came back to Vegas from Tucson. Ended up going to pipefitting school in my forties. By the time I graduated and got my plumbers and pipefitters cards I was fifty.

Now I'm retired; a bad back forced me to. I get a pension from the Culinary Union, I get one from the Plumbers and Pipefitters Union, and I get Social Security.

My sobriety date is January 7, 1997. I celebrated twenty years a couple weeks ago. For my twentieth sobriety birthday I told my nephew, the one who referred me to the veterans hospital in Tucson, "I'm celebrating! Twenty's a big one!"

He said, "We'll be there."

He flew in from Tucson with my sister and her husband. My brother was there and so were a lot of people I met in AA. A DJ came and we danced and sang karaoke. It was a blast!

ANDE

Ande: I had the full right mastectomy. The doctor told me she got all the cancer out. She said, "It doesn't get any better than that." Zero. Nothing.

They gave me a new breast. I couldn't believe it. It was covered by my insurance.

I also got the full teeth reconstruction, eye surgery, and rabies treatment from when I got bit by a desert rat.

Tex: I'm property manager of a wedding venue outside of Houston. It's sixty acres and I live on property in an RV that's got all the amenities of a home. I got my first TV in fifteen years; went and bought me a nice Samsung forty-inch flat screen. I have my own truck.

I do general maintenance. I have horses and cows to take care of. I do plumbing and air conditioning. Plus, during the days, we have weddings and I help the bride and groom if they need anything or have questions about the property.

I have three biological children, two stepchildren, and several grandkids. I'm blessed to be able to spend time with 'em. This is what I said I wanted in the CrowdRise video. This is what I hoped for. When my grandkids look up at me and call me Pawpaw, let me tell you what. That's a weird-sounding word, but it's the greatest in the English language.

I went and visited my mother's grave in North Carolina, and I was cryin' and Marley, who's four, said, "Don't cry, Pawpaw. It's okay. We love you."

For a four-year-old who just met you to be able to look at you with unconditional love and tell you it's gonna be okay, that made me wanna cry even more. I never thought I'd be able to have that. I figured I'd have to see my grandkids grow up in pictures like I'd seen my kids do.

Phil: My life is much slower and more calculated now instead of just wingin' it. I'm settled down with the girl I met on the poker site and am doing with my three stepkids what I should've done with my own two kids. My kids don't resent it though. They sit back and say, "You were just like this in the good times we had together."

I don't terrorize my kids or stepkids with the stories I could tell 'em. I just let 'em know I've been to hell and back at least two or three times. That's all I can do.

I see how beautiful my youngest daughter is. She's nineteen now. I see my granddaughter. I'm thinking, Wow, this is what life is supposed to be like. I'm sittin' in my favorite chair in my house. My kids and grandkids are visiting me. We're laughing.

That's what it's all about. That makes the journey worth it.

LESSONS LEARNED

Few people have endured more fire and rain, literally and figuratively, than the survivors of the Las Vegas storm drains. As Phil said, they've been to hell and back at least two or three times. If it's true that we learn most from our trials and tribulations, from our false starts and abject failures, these individuals must be founts of wisdom.

I wanted to tap that knowledge, the street smarts they developed to survive those dark days and bright nights. Hence the questions: What can others learn from your experience? What advice do you have?

I believe their answers can benefit not only teenagers, recovering addicts, and the homeless, but the population at large.

Melinda: Walk away. Get help. Don't ever think you have to stay. Don't ever think there's no one who can help you. If you have to, go inside a store or mall or church.

There's hope. If you're separated from your kids or dealing with any kind of abuse or addiction, there's always hope.

Tex: If you're sincere in what you wanna do and you really wanna do it, can't nobody or nothing stop you.

Somebody has to give you some help when you're ready for it; you can't do it by yourself. But there's always gonna be someone there to give you help if you're sincere.

There's nothing wrong with asking for help, and once you get it can't nobody stop you but yourself. There's only one person who can mess up my situation: me.

Sweeny: I was too proud and stubborn to let my family help me. If you have family and need help don't be afraid to ask them for it. Keep in contact with your family no matter what.

Jazz: I wish I would've dealt with my issues earlier. Gotten therapy or something. My stepdad abused me and my mom and that had an effect on me.

I also wish I would've gone to school to learn a trade. I regret not having a career.

Jamie: Don't go down this path, man. It leads nowhere, except to death, prison, or a tunnel under the Las Vegas Strip.

Work for a living or whatever, but don't hurt nobody and keep your morals and dignity intact. That's one thing I managed to hang onto, even at my lowest: my dignity. I kept it because I never screwed over anybody I knew or loved.

Pretty Boy Steve: Being homeless isn't an adventure. If you do find yourself on the street get off it as soon as you can. It isn't fun. I've told homeless kids that, but it's already too late for them because they're enjoying the lifestyle. When you're young you don't care; you'll sleep in a tunnel with a few sheets of newspaper over you. As you get older it gets harder to live like that and to get yourself out of the situation.

Cyndi: Treat the homeless like people, not subhumans. Give 'em a sandwich, a bottle of water, a dollar. Talk to 'em. Tell 'em you're gonna say a prayer for 'em. Tell 'em to not give up.

Give 'em some hope. That's what I was given.

Ned: I take time to praise people who need someone or something because that's what they're really lacking. People wanna come down on those who are in a bad spot: "You suck!" "You're a junkie!" "You're a lazy piece of shit!"

Everyone's yelling stuff outta car windows, but no one's pulling over and trying to find out what caused the problem and how they might be able to help. If you ask questions and show some concern and provide encouragement, it may give 'em the fuel they need to find that inner passion to get better.

Religion is not my thing, but I know there's a power that works within each of us that makes us shine. A deep faith. Even in the tunnel, on the gloomiest day, it shined in me. I saw the same thing in Dee.

Keep that light shining. Don't ever let it burn out.

Knyck: We need to tell people, especially kids, the truth about drugs. I think the failure of D.A.R.E. and the War on Drugs is they give this bullshit idea about what drugs are. They make 'em out to be entirely bad. Why would anybody do drugs if they're all bad?

I'd tell kids the truth about drugs: They'll make you feel good and you'll have fun, but you won't give a damn about anything else. Try to make that message as simple and honest as possible.

Practice mindfulness. That's the most important thing to me. If I don't take twenty minutes a day to meditate, just a simple mantra to get in touch with my emotions and the world around me, I'm not present. I think it's necessary to being a human. Otherwise we lack compassion and empathy.

If we're not in touch with ourselves how can we get in touch with others?

Becky: What you put into the universe is what you get back. If you're putting out negativity and evil that's what you'll get in return.

I experienced that. I lived it. I know it to be true.

Vegas Dee: Take a quick look at the situation you're in and realize that current or past afflictions should not dictate the future. Don't let the past or present destroy you. Know your worth and keep looking and moving forward.

Shaggy: Your biggest weakness can become your biggest strength. My weakness, my drug addiction, has become my greatest asset at Freedom House. Clients can relate to me and they listen to me. I'm able to walk them through this process as an equal rather than a superior.

Stephen: Most treatment centers will ask you fifty questions to see if you're an alcoholic. The Big Book only asks two: Can you give up drinking entirely and when you drink can you control the amount?

Those are two questions you might wanna ask yourself. If you can't answer yes to both of 'em you may wanna get some help.

Tommy: Try a twelve-step program if you wanna. It might help. I just didn't think it would work for me. For me there was only one step: Look in the mirror and admit you were a dumbass for the last forty years. When you admit that to yourself it's easy to stop drinking.

I talk about drinking too. I remember the good old days. The other day I was drinking a Monster and I said to a friend, "This would taste really good with a shot of rum in it."

"I thought you didn't drink anymore," he said.

"I don't. I'm just sayin'."

I can't act like alcohol doesn't exist. I think that's why some people go back to drinking: They try to hide or deny it and it overwhelms 'em at some point.

Easy E: They say the first ninety days you shouldn't say nothing at meetings. Bullshit! As soon as you have something to say that you think can help somebody, say it. Don't sit in the corner and drink coffee and wait till the meeting is over and go outside and have a cigarette and talk shit. Don't hang out outside the meeting hall; that's where the vultures are. Hang out inside and join the conversation.

When you're in recovery don't get down on yourself for making a mistake. Addiction is a motherfucker. It's not easy to get it right on the first try. I didn't. I got thrown out thirty-four days into a thirty-five-day program.

Most people don't get it right the first time. You may not get it right the first 100 times, but keep tryin'. Jump right in the next day and go to a meeting, talk to a mentor, try another program. Whatever it takes.

Quitters are the ones who end up back in the tunnels, cold and pale, with a needle hangin' from their arm.

Rick: I tell the guys at Origins as long as a man draws breath there's hope for recovery. It's never too late, there's no bottom too low, there's no hole you can't climb out of.

When I see a man in a hole I jump in with him. He says, "Dude, now we're both stuck."

And I say, "It's okay, brother. I know the way out."

DOWN THE ROAD

What are your hopes for the future? What are your plans?

The preceding chapters gave insight into the storm-drain survivors' past and present. The goal of this chapter, as indicated by the above prompt, is to provide a sense of where they're going.

The responses range from vague to specific, somber to lighthearted, modest to grand. Some of the interviewees plan to take it slow, others intend to take over the world.

Ned: I have a lotta goals, but I have to go slow. I've had extravagant things and what did I do with 'em? Wasted 'em. I drive a Toyota Avalon. It's an old man's car, but it gets me from point A to B.

The guys I work with at the dealership, who are in their twenties, are buying sports cars. Those are nice, but they're not a necessity for me. My goal is to be the best husband I can be to my future wife, the best parent I can be to her little girl, and the best person I can be to myself.

Szmauz: The end goal is to move to Olympia, Washington, with my wonderful partner, Gwen, and live in a tiny house with a bunch of cats and dogs. Olympia has always been a hotspot for me for various reasons. Cobain was the original reason, but so much great stuff happens there. K Records, my favorite record company on the planet, is there. It's got one of the best indie-music scenes in the country. It's where I need to be, man!

Misty: Have a job. Be out of U.S. VETS and on my own. Be back in Oregon. Have Keeper and the rest of my kids grow up happy and healthy.

I'm honest with my children. My daughter Indica is old enough to understand. She had my picture facedown on her nightstand. "I'm mad at you, Mommy. You never come visit me. Are you in timeout?"

"Mommy's sick, honey. I'm doing things I shouldn't do and it's taking time away from you and it's not right. One of these days I'll be better."

I'm hoping that day will come soon.

Knyck: My goal is to have a family with Maddie. She's not like anybody else I've been with. She's trustworthy, loyal. She's perfect. I can't believe she exists.

TK: Become a vet tech, get paid more money, and hopefully have a family. I moved from the tunnels to the streets to the ghetto and now I'm renting a room in a nice house in a nice neighborhood.

Keep moving forward. That's my goal.

Pretty Boy Steve: My hopes are that Kat and I are still together and I'll have some sort of normal job, whether it's part time or full time, and we'll be out of the tunnels. My mind's still sharp. I'm in fairly good health. I'm a little sunburned and I need to get my teeth fixed; they're falling

TK

out all over the place. But I do see better things ahead. They can only get better.

Kat: I want some place that's safe and warm. I want peace. I want light.

Stephen: I got a call outta the blue from a girl I married and divorced thirty years ago.

My nephew from Tucson goes to the White Mountains every Thanksgiving and organizes a family reunion there. My ex drove down with me and we had a great time, but she can't do nothin' with the situation she's in. She's fighting for custody of her kids. But when her kids are grown maybe her and I can get back together. She's the love of my life.

She said, "Leaving you was the biggest mistake I ever made."

I said, "I was a drunk and working at a carwash. I would've left me too."

Ande: I'm gonna continue to heal from the cancer and move to Idaho to take care of Marge, one of the women I fell in love with when I was in my twenties. We got back in touch and have been talking. I hope to also work with the forest rangers in that region, studying the calderas and their possible effect on the environment. That's the best use of my PhD right now, I think.

Becky: Me and my daughter are in Utah and Zero and our son are in Mississippi. I want us all to be together, but I told Zero we can't live near a casino. They mess everything up for us. That's the problem; he's addicted to gambling and he'll never get away from it because he's a casino dealer. If I get an operator job at the ice-cream factory I'm working at, I can take care of both of us and he wouldn't have to work at a casino.

If Zero doesn't forgive me for what I did that's fine. I'll get over it. But I have to be with my son.

Zero: I'll probably be dead. Live fast, die hard, and leave a decent-looking corpse. All I worry about is my son. I have life insurance, so if anything happens to me at least he'll be taken care of.

Jamie: I'll be on a different plane of existence soon. I've got eight stents in my chest. I've had fourteen heart attacks. I've had quadruple-bypass surgery. I got a year or two left tops. My doctors told me I need to look at my "quality of life." That's what they tell people who have six months or less left.

I went into the bypass surgery with a 20 percent chance of survival. There were family members at the hospital who I hadn't seen in years. I was like, What are all these people doing here? The doctors didn't tell me I had only a 20 percent chance of surviving, but when they wheeled me into the operating room I was humming a Blackberry Smoke song. If it was my time I was ready.

One Shoe Sue: I recently told my boss at Dairy Queen that I plan to retire with him. I'd also like to see my grandson grow up and my youngest son graduate from high school. My focus for the next five years is my job, my son's schooling, and AA. I sponsor five girls. I'm very busy right now, which is a good thing. It keeps me out of trouble.

David: I got three granddaughters. One's nine, one's six, and one's three. They're my little princesses. The first thing I taught 'em to do was pray. I'm proud of that. I help 'em with their homework. I pick 'em up from school.

One thing I wanna do is escort my oldest granddaughter on her first date seven or eight years from now. I wanna make sure she's treated right.

My focus is being the best grandfather I can be, and so far I am the best. I haven't seen many grandfathers who are as involved as I am.

Cyndi: I'd like to open a treatment center in Vegas and help people in the tunnels. That's my ultimate dream. I'd walk the tunnels and talk to people and give 'em food and water and clothes. Have a donation drop-off and take stuff down to 'em. If somebody wanted to get sober and get out they could come to the center and get better and become productive members of society.

Shaggy: Recently I was given the opportunity to take on a major role with Shine a Light. The opportunity to lead the program fell into my lap and I seized it because it hits close to home. There will always be a special place in my heart for the time I spent underground and the culture I embraced for those few years. I also remember feeling trapped down there, as if nothing could help me find my way out. I could see only what had been and what was; I was unable to see what could be.

I feel like I've been given the chance to help the people down there and show them there is a light at the end of the tunnel.

Tex: I hope to use the knowledge I'm gaining at the wedding venue. My boss is talking about building new venues and I'd like to be in charge of or a partner in one of 'em.

I also wanna move my children from North Carolina to Texas. That's one of my main objectives: to have my children and grandchildren closer to me.

If I was to die tomorrow at least I know my grandkids got to see me, and my kids know what kinda person I am. I'm not panhandling no more. I'm not stealing. I'm not doing drugs. I've turned my life around and I'm going to heaven.

You can't ask for much more than that.

TEX

Barry: Hit Powerball for $500 million and see which family members come crawling back. Retire from the tree-service company and go for my Class A commercial driver's license and buy a truck and travel the country. Just do long hauling and travel. Go to Maine and take a week off. Go to Washington state, take a week off. That'd be the perfect life for me. I don't have family. I don't have to be home on the weekends with a wife and kids. I only have the two cats and they can go with me.

Tommy: Sitting on a porch swing not doing a damn thing but playing with my dogs.

Jazz: When I'm released from prison I'm gonna get with my girlfriend, Yvette, and talk with her and her mom. Just have some time to decompress and think without having drugs or alcohol around. I don't wanna get high and live in the tunnels. I can't go through that again.

Meth turns me into a monster. I've run up on people on the Strip with a knife. "Why you following me? Get the fuck away!" I hear voices and swear someone's talking about me, but I know it's my own guilty conscience. I torture myself for being homeless, for being an absentee father, for not saving Sharon. I don't wanna have those thoughts anymore. I don't wanna be like that again, a monster and a lost little boy at the same time.

A ladybug flew into my cell last night. Green with black polka dots. I gotta go through three security doors to get into my unit. How that little bug ended up flyin' around in circles above my desk blew me away, but I do believe ladybugs are good luck.

I didn't put him in a jar or nothin'. I just let him be and he was still around in the morning. I put him in my hand and walked out to the yard. When I got there, I opened my hand and he flew away.

IN CONCLUSION

The last question I asked the storm-drain survivors—sometimes after talking for more than two hours—was, Final thoughts? A few of them, no doubt fatigued, declined the invitation, but most made closing statements of sorts. They were a potpourri of philosophical reflections, regrets, affirmations, RIPs, motivational speeches, and moments of gratitude.

Without further ado, and for the final time, I clear the stage.

> **David:** It was mostly by choice that we were in the tunnels. We didn't wanna be beholden to anybody. We wanted to do things on our own terms.
>
> Everyone down there was interesting: Steve, Kat, Phil, Easy E, Sweeny, Manny, Melinda. All of us were above average intelligence and we'd decided we didn't wanna be part of society. That's the one thing we had in common.

> **Ned:** I wasted a lotta years, but I became a stronger individual. I'm not afraid of anything now. I've seen demons. I've seen spiritual beings. It's not the drugs. I believe I opened doors into different realms, and certain things were shown to me.

Whether it was advice or a learning experience I tried to accept it and take it for what it was, and somehow I made it through.

I get stuff thrown at me and I reflect on those times and think, This is gonna be a breeze. I can figure it out.

Misty: I've been raped. I've been sexually abused. I've been beaten up in and outta the drains. I've been on the verge of death, but I'm still here. Obviously someone has a plan for me.

It was my choice to get off the streets. It was my choice, in a lotta ways, to be on 'em. I chose drugs instead of my studies and kids. I could've done so much more, but it was already written. If I could do it differently I wouldn't because I wouldn't have met the people I've met and had the experiences I've had. I wouldn't have four children and another on the way. I wouldn't be sitting here with you doing this interview.

Tommy: If I can come this far—working construction, happily married, two cats and two dogs—think of what I could've done if I'd been clean my whole life. I could be someplace. I'm never going to be where I should be, but I'm a long way from where I was.

Half Pint: I still don't have a nail on those three fingers. It's a constant reminder of where I don't ever wanna go again.

Stephen: I ran into that girl I used to share motel rooms with, the one I really liked, the one who'd disappeared. This was in '98 or '99 and I was one or two years sober. She was a patient at WestCare. She didn't recognize me at first, then she said, "Hey, Steve! How ya doing?"

She was in bad shape and I never saw her again after that. I have no idea if she's dead or alive. She was more addicted to what she did, that whole lifestyle, than the drugs.

One Shoe Sue: Some of the years of my life are blank. God hasn't revealed 'em to me yet.

I wish I could remember certain things, but I didn't walk away from that experience thinking I'd remember it. I'll never forget that Wendy's though and its parking lot and how many hours I spent sitting in it wishing for better things. Watching people pull into the drive-through and thinking, Why am I here? What am I doing? Why am I not in that car living a normal life like that person?

Manny: I'll never forget what I did to Melinda. That scar will stay with me too.

ONE SHOE SUE

Ricky Lee: I try not to regret anything. It'll just bring you down. I don't regret much anyway. I came to a lotta crossroads and I could've taken different turns, but I'd be living a boring life. Doing the nine-to-five thing and coming home to a wife and kids just isn't me. I couldn't handle it. It's the chaos theory. If there isn't enough chaos in my life I'll create some.

Easy E: If I was around any of the old people from the tunnels I'd probably go after 'em with a baseball bat. The past, man, never leaves my head. Now that I'm clean and sober I remember all the shit they did to me and how they used me.

Skip: I was at Catholic Charities and saw the news on TV—a woman drowned in a flood—then someone called and told me it was Sharon. I couldn't believe it.

The night before I had a dream about her. In the dream she gave me some pizza, walked outta the tunnel, and called 911. The paramedics put me on a stretcher and she was watching.

"Don't worry, Skip," she said. "They're gonna help you."

I guess it was God's way of showing me how I got to the hospital. Sharon saved my arm and my life.

Jamie: Every day was an adventure in the tunnels. Literally living hour to hour. It became a joke with Skip, Zero, Ricky Lee, and the rest of us. If someone asked "What are you doing tomorrow?" the answer was always "We don't know what we're doing an hour from now."

There was a real sense of freedom in that.

I remember Sharon saying she had a phobia of drowning. She said she'd hate to drown because you know you're gonna die.

She was a good person, a good soul, a good friend. She didn't try to set nobody on fire or take nobody's stuff. She'd give you what little she had.

The tunnel's a much darker place without her.

Jazz: I miss Sharon so much. I love that woman with all my heart. The nine years we shared were some of the best of my life, even if we were living in a tunnel and running the streets.

It's sad that this world lost her. I beat myself up because of that day. I replay everything in my head. If I'd done this differently or that differently. All the could'ves and should'ves.

Rick: There are times when my old way of thinking comes back and I say to myself, Sobriety sucks! Then I go on YouTube and look at some videos and remember where Cyndi and I came from, what that looked like, what we looked like, all the pitfalls of that lifestyle. I see how far we've come and all the things we have to be grateful for.

Tex: There's that saying about not judging a man till you've walked a mile in his shoes. I walked a mile in 'em and it was a *long* one, but if I had it to do over again I wouldn't change a thing. Being homeless made me a better person. It made me more mature. I was the most self-centered, uncaring, mean motherfucker you could ever meet.

That's what twelve years in a tunnel did: it made me a better person.

Zero: The tunnels were just a resting place. I never felt weird or guilty when I stayed in 'em because I didn't have any responsibilities. I didn't have kids to take care of or worry about. I wasn't even homeless per se. I just like to save money, and I stayed in the tunnels till I didn't need to anymore. I was always in and out of places. When you're doing drugs and gambling you're a prince one day and a pauper the next.

Knyck: There's a war going on against the homeless in Las Vegas. There are cops and CIs all over the Trop and Eastern area and a lot of other neighborhoods. I could give a shit because I'm not doing anything illegal, but most homeless people don't know their rights and they treat 'em like they're not citizens.

TK: The majority of homeless people I've met have mental-health problems. A lot of 'em haven't been diagnosed, so they self-medicate and get lost in the whirlpool of the streets. They need to get diagnosed and get the right meds. I'm not pro meds 'cause they're being forced on people, and pharmacies and drug companies just wanna make money, but some people do need 'em.

We need to do something about the whole mental-health issue, or the homeless problem will only get worse.

Shaggy: I never met a bad person in the tunnels. They were rough around the edges. They were not "normal" by society's standards. But they were good people. I was honored to be a part of it, but it was a bigger honor to get away from it. Being able to escape it allows you to appreciate the experience.

Before I started doing outreach down there I'd visited the tunnels twice: once because it was raining and I helped

SHAGGY

the people save some stuff, the second time because of "graveyards," old campsites you're not supposed to touch. I wanted to see if my camp was still there, and it was: the bed, a wooden nightstand, magazine pictures of Eminem and Metallica. I stood there for ten or fifteen minutes. It was one of the most spiritual moments of my life.

I have a firepit in my back yard and I go out there and start bonfires, like we did in the drains. Every night I throw wood into the pit and stand there and watch it burn.

Phil: I look back on it and think, Holy shit! What was that?

I laugh at these survivor shows on TV. I could show 'em how it's done. Put me on one of those programs and you're gonna be paying me the winner's check at the end.

I can still see it, but it's like a picture; it feels distant. We'd walk into the tunnel and get to the bend and look over our shoulder, and we could see how small the opening is. We could barely see out of it. That's how I see the tunnels now.

Cyndi: When it rains I'm thankful I'm not pulling stuff outta the tunnel, scared about where I'm gonna go and what I'm gonna do. Freezing. Possibly drowning.

After a year at Origins me and Rick got our own apartment, and every year that we've been on South Padre Island we've moved into a better place. We just moved into a house on the ocean side. We can walk out on our back porch and see the beach. We have a roof over our head and a true appreciation for it.

When I walk on the beach I'm in awe. I think about bringing my kids here and sharing it with 'em, having 'em all visit this spiritual vortex and showing 'em the love and peace I've been able to receive from it. Considering everything I've done, I don't deserve the life I have. I don't deserve it, but I am grateful for it.

EPILOGUE

Since the storm-drain survivors have shared their lessons learned, it seems appropriate that I share a few of my own. I've spent more than twenty years writing about the homeless, and more than a decade working with Shine a Light, and this book is the culmination of a three-and-a-half-year passion project; the experience has led me to some hard realizations.

A few disclaimers before I begin: As previously stated, homeless people don't want to live on the streets. If nothing else, I hope these examples of people getting housed and clean illustrate that. Secondly, my observations are shaped by my time in Las Vegas. While I have researched and interacted with homeless populations in many cities, including L.A., Atlanta, New York, Barcelona, and San Salvador, the opinions below do not necessarily apply to places outside of Vegas.

· · · ·

I've met very few sober non-gamblers on the streets and in the drains. In my estimation, more than 90 percent of homeless are addicted to drugs, alcohol, or gambling, or some combination of the three. It can be tough to tell the primary addiction from the secondary one, and many addicts say gambling is their worst habit of all because of the false hope it creates and the 24/7 availability. (Sometimes the dope man goes to sleep or runs out of product.)

The stories in this book support my estimate. Thirty-five of the thirty-six interviewees were addicted to drugs and/or alcohol while living in the drains—fourteen to meth, twelve crack, ten alcohol, and six heroin. (Some of them had multiple addictions.) Barry, the convicted sex offender from Michigan, was the lone non-addict.

However, this does not mean that substance abuse causes people to become homeless. Drugs and alcohol are often used as an escape from the harsh realities of the streets or to drown out childhood trauma.

• • • •

So what causes homelessness? Is it poverty? Mental illness? A lack of affordable housing? Those are possibilities, but what about childhood trauma?

In the mid-nineties, Kaiser Permanente and the Centers for Disease Control and Prevention conducted a joint study on the impacts of childhood trauma. The study surveyed more than 17,000 adults on their exposure to "adverse childhood experiences" (ACEs), including abuse, neglect, mental illness, substance abuse, separation or divorce, and domestic violence. Roughly 67 percent of the participants had been exposed to at least one ACE and 13 percent had been exposed to four or more.

The study connected the number of ACEs an individual had to high-risk behaviors later in life, like smoking, substance abuse, and promiscuity, as well as to social and health problems, such as depression, PTSD, and cancer. In short, it connected adverse childhood experiences to behaviors and issues associated with homelessness.

Looking at this book through the lens of the *Adverse Childhood Experiences Study*, I can't help but notice that most of the storm-drain survivors had one or more ACEs. Many had four or more.

Maddie and Vegas Dee shared tales of child abuse. Zero, Half Pint, and Melinda spoke of neglect. Becky, Misty, Shaggy, and others were exposed to substance abuse. Ned, Melinda, Misty, et al. suffered through parental separation or divorce. Misty, Stephen, and Vegas Dee witnessed domestic violence. Some of the experiences were so traumatic they defy the study's categorization: Four Finger Mike's shop-class incident, the accidental shooting death of Iron's high school girlfriend, the sudden death of Cyndi's baby brother and her father's subsequent suicide.

Dr. Robert Block, the former president of the American Academy of Pediatrics, is often quoted as saying, "Adverse childhood experiences are the single greatest unaddressed public health threat facing our nation." They are also, perhaps, one of the most overlooked causes of homelessness.

. . . .

Every year, communities across the United States conduct a homeless census. These local numbers are used by the Department of Housing and Urban Development to arrive at its annual national count. HUD's 2019 count, referenced in the "Earliest Memory" chapter, was 568,000. The actual number may be more than a million.

I've participated in the Southern Nevada homeless census and, while well meaning, it's a bit of a farce. It takes place late on a weekday night in January, which discourages volunteers; those who do show up are asked to cover a large tract of land in a short window of time. At night in January, the homeless are burrowed in and less visible, or even temporarily staying in a weekly or a friend's apartment.

The 2019 Clark County census identified 5,300 homeless, the lowest number in the twelve-year history of the count. My eyes and experience tell me the actual number is more than 10,000. In central Vegas, homeless congregate at nearly every park, intersection, convenience store, drug store, and fast-food restaurant. They're a fixture in the suburbs, too. And those are just the visible homeless. The goal of many street people is to remain invisible—out of sight, out of the police cruiser. Hence the proliferation of people living in abandoned buildings, vacant homes, underground flood channels, on undeveloped dirt lots, and in other places that the census workers can't cover in one night.

Four hundred communities participate in HUD's annual homeless count. They follow the same procedure as Clark County—surveying large swaths of urban terrain on one late January night—and are similarly limited in scope. Thus a personal rule regarding the counts, whether tallying 5,000 or 500,000: double the number and you'll be closer to the truth.

· · · ·

Six days a week, Eric, who used to live in a drain near the Orleans, climbed on his bike and pedaled his recycling route. He'd sort the haul, most of it procured by dumpster-diving, in the tunnel, then bike it to a recycling center. He worked fifteen hours a day and made about $100.

PRETTY BOY STEVE AND KAT

His tunnel neighbor Charlie worked full time at an auto shop.

"Everyone in that tunnel worked hard," says Eric, who's now housed and employed in Texas.

In addition to their work, Eric and Charlie had to avoid the cops, keep their camps clean, and prepare for floods. All of this, oftentimes, in extreme temperatures.

Many of the interviewees exhibited this same grit and work ethic. Pretty Boy Steve and Kat, with their diligent homemaking and dedication to credit hustling, come to mind. Eddie found and maintained a job as a forklift operator, allowing him and Jodie to move into a weekly. Ned perfected the art of selling nightclub passes.

Call the homeless what you will, but don't call them lazy. They're the most industrious people I've met. Their survival depends on it.

. . . .

I once assumed that it took thousands of dollars to help a homeless person. What I've learned through Shine a Light and these interviews is that small things can have a big impact on the homeless. Introduce yourself, shake their hand (no matter how dirty it is), ask how their day is going. Don't lecture them; they've heard enough of that from friends, family, police, and politicians. Don't bullshit them; their detectors are fine tuned. Don't give them money; that's lazy and impersonal and it may feed an addiction. Be positive. Encourage them. Buy them a nonalcoholic drink, a meal, or flowers. Keep bottled water, snacks, socks, and underwear in your car and offer them those.

The homeless are uniquely appreciative, and I've seen small acts such as these lift their spirits and bolster their confidence. They can even inspire them to make a change.

Matthew O'Brien
April 2020

ACKNOWLEDGMENTS

Thank you to the interviewees.

Thanks to my mom Liz and dad Matt, my sisters Cathy and Leslie and brother Eric, my brothers-in-law Peter Gwin and Tyler Gibbs and sister-in-law Emily and her dad Rowland LeMaster, my nieces Eliza, Julia, and Belle and nephews Ellis, Tim, and Chapman.

Thanks, Josh Ellis, Steve Fanell, Jarret Keene, and Chris Staros.

Thanks, Dan Hernandez, Patrick Hughes, Valerie Killeen, Nancy Schenck, and the entire Central Recovery Press staff.

And thanks, Deke Castleman, Tod Goldberg, Arely Gramajo, Hudak Hendrix, Stacy Mattingly, Tim O'Grady, Cathy Scott, and David Sweetland.

GLOSSARY

Bone out - leave

Boost - steal

Booster - thief

CI - confidential informant

CPS - Child Protective Services

Cop - get, get high

Credit hustle - look for or steal credits from slot machines

D-Boy - drug dealer

DTs - delirium tremens; a condition of alcohol withdrawal involving tremors and hallucinations

Eight-ball - one-eighth of an ounce of drugs

Fly a sign - hold up a sign that solicits money

GTA - grand theft auto

HELP of Southern Nevada - Las Vegas-based nonprofit that serves the poor and homeless

Hooch - shelter, improvised dwelling

John - male client of a female prostitute

Lick - goods or money obtained quickly

Obama phone - free phone given to the poor and homeless by the U.S. government

Road dog - close friend, running mate

Run and gun - hustle the streets in a fast, reckless manner

Run the rail - inhale an entire line of meth or coke

Sack - small bag of drugs

Scabby - despicable, loathsome

Score - procure drugs

Scrap - recycle scrap metal

Shiesty - suspicious, untrustworthy

Shine a Light - community project founded by Matthew O'Brien to help the people in the drains

Spange - beg for spare change

Strapped - armed with a weapon

Stretch - prison sentence

The Big Book - *Alcoholics Anonymous*

Turn tricks - work as a prostitute

UA - urinalysis

U.S. VETS - national nonprofit that provides services to homeless veterans

Veterans Village - transitional and permanent housing for veterans and others

Weekly - weekly motel

WestCare - national nonprofit that offers behavioral health and human services, including detox

Wigger - white person who appropriates black culture

Xanie bar - two-milligram Xanax pill that's bar-shaped